10 LIES
MEN BELIEVE ABOUT
PORN

STEPHEN KUHN

Morgan James Publishing
New York

All emphasis (italics) in Scripture verses has been added by the author.

10 LIES MEN BELIEVE ABOUT PORN

ISBN 978-1-6304-7030-2 Paperback
ISBN 978-1-6304-7031-9 eBook
ISBN 978-1-6304-7032-6 Hardcover
ISBN 978-1-6304-7095-1 Audio
Library of Congress Control Number: 2013957756

Cover and Interior design by Stephen Kuhn

Cover photo: *The Judgement of Paris,* Peter Paul Rubens. C. 1636 (National Gallery, London). Image taken from Wikimedia Commons: http://en.wikipedia.org/wiki/Judgement_of_Paris

Published in New York, New York, by Morgan James Publishing. Morgan James and The Entrepreneurial Publisher are trademarks of Morgan James, LLC. www.MorganJamesPublishing.com

To the wife of my youth.

I will love you…

Always

Contents

There is something more than a little disconcerting about writing your own autobiography. When people have occasionally asked me what I am working on, I have found it impossible to tell them without an inward blush.

As if anybody cares or should care...

But I do it anyway. I do it because it seems to me that no matter who you are, and no matter how eloquent or otherwise, if you tell your own story with sufficient candor and concreteness, it will be an interesting story and in some sense a universal story...

If God speaks to us at all other than through such official channels as the Bible and the church, then I think that He speaks to us largely through what happens to us, so what I have done in this book is to listen back over what has happened to me—as I hope my readers may be moved to listen back over what has happened to them—for the sound, above all else, of His voice...

For His word to us is both recoverable and precious beyond telling.

— **FREDERICK BUECHNER** —

INTRODUCTION

I Have a Confession...

You know, I've got a confession to make myself.
I'm not really a priest, I've just got my shirt on backwards.

RYAN STILES

I have a confession to make. Up until a few years ago, I was single-handedly keeping the multibillion-dollar pornography industry alive. I don't quite know how the numbers all added up, but it had to be true. The way I figured it, I was the only guy with a pornography problem from what I could tell. I know none of my friends struggled with it, that's for sure. And it surely wasn't an issue for the other men in my church. I was the only man in the sanctuary, I thought, the only man in the world trying to fight this battle.

> *What kind of believer am I anyway? Not a very good one, obviously. God must be so ashamed of me. Why can't I get it together? Why am I failing so badly at following Jesus?*

I was sitting in church most Sundays, unable to close my eyes during prayer for fear of what would pop into my head from the polluted corners of my mind.

What will others think if they find out I have this secret? What if they find out how far away from God I really am? There's no way I can tell them the truth about me.

I thought my struggle with porn would all go away when I got married, but somehow it actually got worse.

What if my wife finds out? It will destroy her. She might leave me. She probably will leave me. I shouldn't tell her. I can't tell her. That would be stupid. We'll be happier if I just keep this hidden and fight it alone. She knows something is wrong, but she doesn't know what it is. I'll fix it, and then things will get better between us. She will never have to know.

I wasn't ready to admit that my struggle had become an addiction. I knew porn controlled my life, but I still saw it as a manageable problem. It was nothing I couldn't handle. I just needed to find the right program, or combination of programs...something had to work.

If I just try harder, find a better Internet filter, or make enough promises to God and to myself, I will eventually find freedom from this. I know I can get it under control eventually...

Nothing is working. I'm getting worse.

Where is God? Why won't He help me?

■ ■ ■

Could these thoughts have gone through your mind as well? I'm willing to bet, if you are reading this book, you've at least thought something similar. The more I have the honor of helping other men find their freedom from pornography addiction, the more I see a consistent pattern of thoughts such as these that are contributing to their bondage. These thoughts are present in almost every case of pornography addiction I have seen, or any habitual sin for that matter.

These thoughts are all lies. Hopefully, by the time you reach the end of this book, you will be aware of not only how to recognize these lies, but more importantly, you will understand the Truth that will set you free from them.

As you read further, you may notice a few things in this book are different from the majority of other books about overcoming addiction. First, I'm not going to give you a bunch of reasons why you shouldn't be looking at porn. I'm not going to develop an in-depth theological treatise on why porn is bad. The last thing you need as a man struggling with pornography is more shame and guilt laid on you. I trust that the Holy Spirit has been convicting you of what may need to change in your life and will continue to make His path clear to you. You are reading a book on finding freedom from pornography, so I assume you have already decided you no longer want porn to be a part of your life—or you are at least considering that decision.

Second, this isn't another to-do book, telling you what you need to do to change your life. This is a what-is-done book, telling you what has already been done in you. Once you begin to see what the Bible says is true regarding these common lies—lies you may be believing about who God is, the work Jesus has done, and who you are in Christ—God's power and life will become alive in you like never before. The bondage in your life will be shattered, blossoming into a relationship of unbelievable freedom.

If there existed three easy steps to freedom that all started with the letter "J" or some clever acrostic for the word "freedom" that outlined a set path to follow, you could apply them to your life without even talking to God about it. But these formulas remove the relationship. Furthermore, God rarely heals two people in the same way. Just look at how Jesus healed the various blind people and lepers in the Gospels. Good luck finding a pattern there. We need to allow God to be creative with us and follow His leading even if we don't have all the answers up front.

Most recovery books are filed under the category of "Self-Help," but lasting change cannot come from trying to help yourself. As long as you are attempting to gain control of your life under your own power and following your own plan, you will continue to struggle. In order to find true and lasting freedom, not just from pornography, but for the deepest needs of your soul, you must start looking in the "God, Help Me" section of the bookstore. I am sure you have fought a valiant fight so far, but this battle belongs to the Lord, not to you.

The majority of this book will focus on what I have found to be the ten most common lies men believe about themselves, about God, and about pornography. These are the lies that are keeping men trapped in bondage. If you can come to believe and understand what the Bible says is true in each of these areas, Satan's power over you will be broken. My life has been completely changed through these truths, and I believe the same can happen for you as well.

There is hope. Freedom is possible. Don't give up yet.

> *"Come to me, all of you who are weary and carry heavy burdens, and I will give you rest. Take my yoke upon you. Let me teach you, because I am humble and gentle at heart, and you will find rest for your souls. For my yoke is easy to bear, and the burden I give you is light."*
>
> — **JESUS CHRIST**[1] —

Choose Your Own Adventure

This book is written under the assumption that you believe in Jesus and have already trusted Him with your life. If that is the case, go ahead and read straight through as you would with any other book. If you are coming into this book from a different worldview, though, and are perhaps only "kicking the tires" of following Jesus, then I encourage you to take a slightly different approach. I suggest you read "My Story" and then skip ahead to Lie #4 and Lie #5 before returning to the beginning. Why? Unless you are in a position of trusting Christ with your life and understand what it means to accept His forgiveness, the first few chapters won't make a lot of sense to you.

Either way, I'm glad you are here, regardless of where you are coming from.

---

1 Matthew 11:28-30.

MY STORY

How I Went from Living a Lie to a Life Worth Living

This is the story all about how
My life got flipped, turned upside down...

FRESH PRINCE OF BEL AIR

I am about to tell you my story for three reasons. First, to show you I am a deeply flawed human just like everyone else. The sin and pain I am capable of producing is astounding. Likewise, my ability to deceive myself into ignoring and justifying my issues is equally shocking. It would seem I have no business writing a book advising anybody of anything. Nonetheless, here I am.

Second, there is a lot of healing that comes from the honest telling of our stories, both for the storyteller and for the audience. I have found over the years of telling my story that we really aren't all that different. As you read the slow motion, instant replay of the highlights (and low-lights) in my journey, I hope you are able to see glimpses of your own story. The details will be different, but the themes will likely be similar in spots. Remember, you are not alone in this struggle.

Finally, I tell you my story to give you a sense of hope as you live out your own story, no matter what chapter you are living in today. If God can use a man such as me in His kingdom, not just in spite of my sordid past, but *because* of my sordid past, think of what He can do with you!

The Spark

I still remember the first time my eyes were opened to what became my drug of choice. I was no older than 12, exploring the woods on my bike with a few friends. We would frequently ride these trails behind the college football stadium and build jumps. Epic jumps. It felt like we were flying six feet in the air, though I'm sure it was only six inches, if that.

Even now I only want to talk about the bikes and jumps and steer the conversation away from the issue of the magazine. It's tempting to make small talk and never allow anyone below the surface—I think it's a guy thing. How about those Seahawks? That Russell Wilson looks like he may just work out for them, huh?

Anyway, we stumbled across a homeless camp one afternoon. No one was home at the time, so as any adventurous middle-school boys would do, we started to explore. Who knew what treasures we would find? There were empty beer cans, broken bottles, and a soggy sleeping bag sitting outside by a fire ring. But the end of the rainbow seemed to be shining upon the weathered orange tent. We cautiously unzipped it, scared that it might have somebody sleeping inside, but found it empty…almost. Just inside the door of the tent was the object that begins this type of story for many men of my generation: a *Playboy* magazine.

I'm not sure if any of us had ever seen a naked woman before we found the magazine. I never had. I had developed plenty of crushes and the normal adolescent curiosities, but I really had no idea what existed beneath the mysterious layers of clothing women always had on. I knew there was something I wanted to see but had never had the opportunity.

Somehow I ended up getting to keep the magazine. I think it was something similar to Gollum wresting the ring from the hands of Frodo, but that may be an exaggeration. All I know for sure is it ended up hidden deep within my closet, and a lifestyle of hiding, lying, deception, and lust had suddenly sunk deep roots into my soul.

Fueling the Fire

I look back now and can't see a moment where I wasn't addicted to porn. I believe for me it began the instant I laid eyes on that magazine. There are numerous reasons for this that are starting to make a lot of sense as I put the pieces back together in my mind. First, God has made me intensely visual. I am a designer by trade and have always been drawn toward visual beauty. I see colors, textures, details, and shapes on a deeper level than most people. You can imagine the effect this has on my appreciation of the female form. The other reason, which is subtler but more influential, was how I viewed myself during that moment of discovery.

I was an awkward kid—chubby, pimply, and nerdy. I would spend my lunch hours hiding in the school library reading *Black Belt* magazine even though I had no martial arts training whatsoever. I guess I thought if I could order the throwing stars from the catalog in the back I would suddenly be cool or something. I wasn't all that popular with the ladies. Maybe I would have been, but I had convinced myself that girls wouldn't like me, so I avoided them to eliminate any opportunities for rejection. If I never talk to them, they can't say no, right?

So there I was, lonely, intensely visual, pubescent hormones raging, scared of female rejection, and finally in possession of what I thought was a "solution." The women in this magazine would never reject me. They didn't care what I looked like. They didn't mind my nerdiness. They would be there to satisfy all my curiosities, my sexual needs, and even my deep desire for human connection. These were all lies of course—the magazine wasn't doing any of this—but I believed them...big time.

Fanning the Flames

Throughout the rest of my teenage years I would come across many more magazines and even a few videos. Usually these would come from friends with older brothers who could legally purchase them for us, but commonly through shoplifting as well. I always felt that porn was wrong, but I didn't really know why. I sensed it was something to keep hidden, knew it was unacceptable in our house, and knew God didn't want me to look at it. I ended up with a pretty good stash regardless, but I always felt like I needed more. I think I sensed from early on there was always something missing. Something better. I just needed to keep looking and eventually I would find it.

By my senior year of high school I had grown out of my awkwardness and girls started to show some interest in me. Because of my pornography habit, I had no idea how to relate to them outside of my self-focused sexuality, so most of my relationships quickly became physical. I had never developed an understanding of God's plan for sexuality, and just hearing "Don't have sex until you're married" wasn't going to cut it. In all honesty, even though I said I wanted to wait, my deepest desire was for sex. God was no longer controlling my life, my sexuality was.

Gasoline on a Dumpster Fire

The first big turning point in my struggle with pornography came when I left for college. It wasn't a turn for the better. Leaving for college ushered me into a new life of independence, a lack of accountability—and unhindered access to the Internet. When I was at home, I was limited to whatever magazines I could find and always at risk of my parents walking in on me. At college I could surf the Internet for porn whenever I wanted…and I did. I would find myself mindlessly surfing porn until three or four in the morning, having no idea where the time had gone. My desire to find the perfect girl or website consumed me.

My addiction had reached a point where I couldn't even make it through my shift delivering pizzas without stopping at the adult bookstore to watch a movie clip in the preview booth. I began pursuing girls I had no interest in having a relationship with outside of sex. Luckily, I rarely had the success in one-night stands I was hoping for. I can now see that God was protecting me from completely destroying myself during those days.

Deep down, I hated what I was doing. I hated how I was being controlled by this sin. I wanted to walk with God and be a "good" guy. I wanted to marry a great girl, be a godly husband, and raise my kids to hopefully love Jesus someday. But I also knew my life was not heading toward those goals—it was moving further away from them. I wanted desperately to be free from this addiction, but I wasn't willing to admit I needed help yet.

I still believed that if I tried hard enough, I could eventually get it under control on my own.

Led Astray from the Wife of My Youth[1]

I met the woman of my dreams during my senior year of college. She was the pure, innocent, Jesus-loving girl I had always dreamed of. She made me want to be the kind of man she actually deserved. By the grace of God, she had enough willpower for the both of us and we dated without giving in to the physical temptations that had plagued my previous relationships. This gave us a beautiful opportunity to grow in our love for each other without the distractions and false intimacy that comes from sex outside of marriage...or so she thought. She was more than I ever could have asked for, and when I finally asked her to marry me, she said yes.

When we married in 2004, she thought she was marrying the man of her dreams because I only allowed her to see the parts of me that were good enough to fit within that image. I never told her about my addiction to pornography. I believed the lie that my addiction would go away when we were married. I believed it would no longer be an issue once we could be physical whenever we wanted, so why would I bring it up and stir the pot? Unfortunately, my addiction actually became worse once we settled into married life.

My wife kept trying to love me and be a good wife, but she had no idea our marriage was doomed from the start. She had married a man who didn't exist. As long as I was pretending to be "perfect Steve," the real me couldn't offer her my love or even receive love from her. Because of this, we never developed the deep intimacy that is required for a marriage to survive, let alone thrive. We continued to grow further and further apart.

I kept spiraling deeper and deeper into the pit of my addiction. I would sense continual rejection from her, not from anything she was doing, but from me secretly knowing she wasn't loving the real me. This imagined rejection caused me to become increasingly fearful of sharing my true self with her, which caused me to retreat into the world of my addiction, where I

1 See Proverbs 5 for an explanation of why I use this phrase.

felt I was safe from rejection. After giving into my addiction again, I would feel so much shame and guilt, knowing that I was letting her down. I was scared of how much it would hurt her if she discovered what I was doing, so I continued to hide that part of myself from her.

My addiction drove me to become a pathological liar. When my wife would ask me what something had cost I'd tell her it was $5 when really it was $6, even though it didn't matter either way. I'd lie to my friends, my parents, my boss, everyone. I'd exaggerate things in conversations for no apparent reason. I even acted as if I was a bad liar with little things so my wife would believe I couldn't lie about the big stuff. If the truth might be damaging for me, I would lie about it without an ounce of guilt. It eventually became more natural for me to be dishonest than honest.

When my wife and I were together, I was present physically but distant mentally. I would frequently zone out, missing her questions and comments. It was as if I weren't even in the same room. I had developed a deeper sense of connection with the computer than with my wife. Ridiculous? This actually makes sense when you think about it. The computer was where I had been going to attempt to fulfill my desires for intimacy and connection, not my wife. Because of this, I would come home and retreat to the study to avoid connecting with her any more than necessary. Connecting with my wife meant the possible risk of rejection or discovery, both of which scared me to the core. So I would sit in front of the computer and surf Facebook or eBay, not looking at anything "wrong," but mindlessly killing time to avoid engaging her. I had put up these walls and barriers to protect me from having to risk myself with her.

Every time we came together physically, I felt immense guilt and shame, which kept me from connecting with her without feeling as if I was doing something wrong. The shame from my sin had penetrated my heart to the point that something which God created as good was distorted in my mind into something that felt shameful. I could no longer distinguish the redeemed, holy sexuality between me and my wife from my sinful sexual addiction. I would desire to be close to her and would flirt with her throughout the day, but once we ended up in the bedroom my shame took over and I would find excuses to pull away. She often asked what was wrong, but because I wasn't willing to admit I knew what the problem was, she assumed there must have been something wrong with her. After all, it was only natural for her to blame herself in the absence of any real answer from me.

You would think that seeing the terrible effects of my sin on my wife would cause me to turn from it, but that unfortunately was not the case. I had reached a point where the most important thing to me was my own protection, even at the risk of hurting others. I had been justifying, lying, hiding, and manipulating for so long that I had completely lost the ability to sense or care about anyone's emotions but my own. I no longer had the ability to feel empathy. I could sit and watch my wife cry herself to sleep and think "she's just being irrational," or "she'll get over it." Every now and then I would wonder if there was something wrong with me because I didn't feel emotions, but I would quickly brush it off. I had no idea how destructive my life had truly become.

The First of Many Turning Points

The first real turning point in my journey came when we found out we were going to have a daughter. Although the thought of hurting my wife wasn't enough for me to seek help, for some reason the thought of hurting my baby girl was. I was listening to a podcast on being a godly father and the preacher was talking about the effects of pornography on a family. He warned that if a father has a porn addiction, he will most likely pull away from his daughter once she reaches puberty because he will feel dirty and shameful if he gives her affection after she starts to mature physically. This pulling away often causes the daughter to feel rejection and start looking for affection elsewhere—often in the arms of a teenage boy who is noticing how she is changing physically as well. I immediately thought of how many of the girls I had dated over the years had absent or distant fathers, and the kind of physical relationships we had. This scared me to death.

A few months after my daughter was born I came across a book called *The Bondage Breaker*. I was skeptical about it at first because it was different from all the other books I had read on the subject. I continued to read it, though, and started to believe what the author was saying might actually be true. I began to understand how my addiction was the result of me not understanding what it meant to have Christ living within me. I had believed lies about my sin—and myself—and these lies were contributing to my bondage. If I would allow God to clear up those lies and show me the truth, freedom would come.

I came to realize that the true nature of my addiction was spiritual, not physical, and I would never be able to find freedom by myself. I followed the prayers of repentance in the book as they guided me through a process of handing my sin over to God and trusting Him to break the chains that had shackled me for so many years. It took many hours as God brought to mind countless acts of sin that had contributed to my bondage. It was the first time I reached out to God for help with my addiction using His power, not my own.

The moment I finished praying, something felt different. I really can't explain it. I started to realize that I no longer felt drawn to the computer in the same way as before. I'd go check my e-mail and Facebook, but even though my wife was gone and I was alone, I didn't feel the urge to look at porn. When I'd wake up the following morning, I would still have no desire to look at porn, even though my usual pattern was to go straight to the computer first thing. I started to believe this *Bondage Breaker* thing might have actually worked. I gave it a few more weeks to be sure my addiction was truly gone and could hardly believe it when I realized it was.

The best part of all of this, or so I thought, was now I would never need to tell my wife. In my mind, the problem had now been taken care of.

God had another plan, though.

My Internet History Hits the Fan

With my newfound freedom, I apparently let my guard down. A few weeks later my wife discovered some questionable things in my Internet history. I believe God had nudged her to start digging, as it had been well over a month since I had last viewed porn. He knew He couldn't let me coast along in life from that point and never fully deal with everything that needed to be addressed in my life. There were still a lot of things He needed to teach me, and I was only just beginning to trust Him with parts of my life.

When my wife confronted me about my Internet history, I finally decided to stop hiding. I confessed my addiction to her. It was an odd moment for me because I was excited to be experiencing this new freedom and wanted her to be excited along with me—but it didn't go over as well as I had hoped. My confession was like a bomb going off in her heart. Everything she thought she knew about me—and our marriage—had been a lie. She felt hurt, betrayed, blindsided, and angry. She asked me how I could have lied to her for so many years knowing full well the damage it was causing. I didn't have an answer for her.

The next few months were really hard for both of us, but for different reasons. My wife was figuring out how to live with and process this new pain, and I began wrestling with God. We began counseling and attempted to find a way to repair the damage I had caused. Our counseling sessions were all the same, though. I would play the part of the victim, saying how I was better now and had come clean. My wife just needed to forgive me so we could move on and live happily ever after. She would respond that she couldn't trust me, didn't see any changes in me, and felt trapped because she didn't know if she was supposed to stay with me or not.

The truth is, she was right about not trusting me. I hadn't built up the courage to face the full extent of my problem yet and was still hiding the worst details of my sin from her. I had cheated on her, but was too much of a coward to confess it to her, so I continued to lie. I told her over and over that I had confessed everything even though I hadn't. I think she wanted to believe me, but God wasn't going to let her. He loved her too much to let her return to a marriage built on a foundation of dishonesty and lies. We eventually decided to stop the counseling because it didn't seem to be making any difference. We had been attempting to fix the symptoms while I was ignoring the much deeper issue. Until I chose to come clean, stop lying, and confess everything to her, nothing was going to change in our marriage.

During this time, I plugged in to a pornography recovery group at a local church as an attempt to show my wife how serious I was about moving toward God and recovery. Even though my motives for joining were wrong, God used the group to keep drawing me closer to Him. I began to realize I wasn't the only man who struggled with sexual sin. I found a community of men who loved me and accepted me even though I still had all sorts of junk in my life. I never felt as if I needed to pretend to be anyone other than who I really was with these men. It was amazing. I would often break down and cry in front of them, and they would do the same in front of me. In all my years of attending church I had never experienced community and fellowship quite like this. Through these relationships, I began to realize that God viewed me this way as well. I had bought into the lie that my sin had continued to separate me from Him and I needed to get it under control before I could have a relationship with Him. In reality, He was right there all along, waiting for me to accept the freedom only He could bring.

Although God was drawing me closer to Him, I continued to dig in my heels on confessing everything to my wife. I still believed that I could lie or bluff my way out of any situation, and with enough time, it would all just be swept under the rug. I figured if I held out long enough, things would finally blow over and get better. This feeling of being in control of my life was completely shattered when my wife finally asked me to move out. It was the moment I knew there was a good chance our marriage wasn't going to be patched up so easily this time.

Breaking Point

By this time, I had been wrestling with God for months about a full confession to my wife. I continued to lie even though I knew I needed to tell her everything. I frequently tried to pray about the situation, hoping for a different answer, but every time I closed my eyes to pray I only heard, *Tell her. Tell her. Tell her.* The still, small voice of God had become a shout—a ringing in my ear that wouldn't go away. I argued with Him—*If I tell her everything, she will leave me.* I would never have said it out loud, but I felt I knew how to manage this situation better than He did.

The breaking point for me was when God showed me how my wife would never be free from the spiritual bondage in her life unless I confessed my adultery to her. Because we were "one flesh," the sins I had committed with my body had also created bondage in her as well. She needed to be made aware of the full truth behind the pain I had caused her so she could know what she needed to be healed from. Something was robbing her of her joy. She needed to know what it was. Even if it meant she would leave me, I knew I had to confess everything to her for her own good. For the first time in our marriage, I was starting to consider putting her well-being above my own desires.

The next morning, my pastor preached on how God is often calling us to do one specific thing at any moment, and walking in holiness is choosing to respond to His call in that moment. I began weeping in church that morning because I knew exactly what I needed to do. God had orchestrated this moment. It was a kick in the pants to get me to stop delaying and to do what I knew He was calling me to do. As I walked out of the sanctuary, I told my pastor I needed to confess some things to my wife, and I made an appointment to meet with him that afternoon so he could make sure I went through with it. I went home and wrote a letter outlining everything I had held back and delivered it to her that morning. I told her how much I loved her, how sorry I was for all the pain I had caused her, and how I knew this would most likely be the end of our marriage. It was the hardest thing I have ever done.

I was convinced that handing that letter to my wife would be the end of all happiness for me. Instead, it became the act of submission that opened the floodgates of God's freedom and mercy in my life. As hard as it was to finally face the full extent of the pain I had caused my wife, it was that moment when I laid my entire life upon the altar and told God, "Whatever you ask of me, whatever you want from me, it's yours. I cannot control things in my life. I am incapable of doing anything good on my own. Even if it costs me everything…I'm all in." I had reached the end of my rope, and God was there to catch me. In that moment, God became real to me for the first time in my life.

Handing My Life Over to God

It has now been over three years since I stopped fighting God and finally allowed Him to take control of my life. It hasn't all been rainbows and kittens—there have definitely been a lot of hard moments—but I wouldn't trade this new life in Christ for anything. By handing over the reins of my life to God, I began to experience what Jesus meant when He said, "My yoke is easy and my burden is light."[2] I've realized that God has always been in control—I was only wasting energy and exhausting myself whenever I tried to wrestle the control from Him. There's something about knowing I don't have the power to actually change anything—and being able to trust that He will take care of things for me—that brings an unbelievable amount of peace and freedom to my life.

I felt Him leading me to start a recovery group in my own church and to come alongside other men in their struggles. I honestly felt like I had no idea how to help other men, but God kept making it clear to me it was what He wanted me to do. Our group has now been meeting for a few years, and I am constantly humbled at how God continues to bring men into my life to walk beside. It's a frequent reminder of how I am not now, and never was, alone in this struggle. Seeing these men start to experience their own freedom in Christ and allowing God's light and love to shine on them is one of the greatest blessings in my life.

As I study the Scriptures and seek after God, He continues to give a deeper understanding of what led to my addiction. He also has shown me why He didn't free me from it when I was in college and first started to see the problems it was causing in my life. If He had rescued me while I was still relying on my own power, I would have attributed my recovery to my own abilities. Being the stubborn man I am, it took me almost 20 years to come face-to-face with my own inability, and God had to let me come to the point of complete brokenness before I would look to Him alone for the answers.

My wife eventually did file for divorce, which was no longer a shock to me at that point. I knew she had no choice. I lost the majority of my savings because of the divorce, as well as through the desire to make amends with people I had stolen from over the years. To top it all off, I also lost my job. I wondered why God was taking everything away from me even though I was following Him fully for the first time in my life. I felt like Job at times, but now I understand what he meant when he said:

> "I had only heard about you before, but now I have seen you with my own eyes" (Job 42:5).

---

2 Matthew 11:30 NIV.

By taking everything from me, God was helping me recognize that all I ever needed was Him. He was allowing me to experience what He means when He says He will never leave me. I could lose everything in my life, but I would never lose Him. He was stripping my life down to its foundation so He could rebuild me exactly as He wanted. His peace was always with me through all of this, and it was amazing how relaxed I felt knowing He was still in control.

New Life in Christ

In that moment of surrender, I finally stepped aside and allowed God to change me into the person He wanted me to be. Once I got out of His way, the changes were astounding. I still have the same personality and mannerisms, but the deepest desires of my heart have been transformed. I no longer have to fight the constant temptation of sin because sin is no longer my greatest desire. It has been replaced by a desire to love others with the love of Christ. My default reaction is to pray for those who hurt me and respond to them in love, not anger or any of the other negative emotions I would have had in the past. It's real, honest love for them. And it just happens naturally. I no longer see money as a means to comfort and security, but see it as a tool to meet the needs of others. I don't need to force myself to read the Bible or pray out of religious duty. Because I have experienced God's deep desire to have a relationship with me, I cannot wait to spend time with Him any opportunity I get.

It's also because of this new life within me that I continue to love and pray for my wife. If I were still the same person as before, but with a shiny new coat of paint, it wouldn't make any sense to wait for her. Why would we attempt to rebuild a marriage that failed so miserably? Wouldn't we just be setting ourselves up for more heartache? The reason I have hope things could be different now is because I know I am no longer the same person. The two of us would be the same people on the outside, but completely new people on the inside. I believe that God can someday show her that I am a new person and heal her heart to a point where she might be open to trusting the work of Christ within me. As much as I desire to be reconciled to my wife, though, I also see how God is using me in this season of singleness. I've come to trust that God knows what's best for me and always has me exactly where He wants me.

I could tell you many stories of how God has provided for me financially, emotionally, and spiritually in these past few years. His blessings continue to blow my mind daily. It becomes easier and easier to trust Him because of the myriad of ways I have seen Him consistently come through. When I look at the frustration of trying to control life on my terms and compare it to the peace and rest that comes from trusting His plan and direction for me, I cannot comprehend how I resisted Him for so long.

No Regrets

I've found that going all-in for Christ is a lot like taking the red pill in *The Matrix*. You suddenly wake up and realize the world you thought was real was actually a lie, and you now get an opportunity to experience real life for the first time. Unlike in *The Matrix*, though, the real world is not dark and depressing, but full of life, love, and joy. One thing is the same—the only way to experience this is to commit to it fully. You have to be all in or it will not work. And once you're all in, there's no turning back.

But I believe you won't want to.

KNOW THINE ENEMY

You Have a Very Real Adversary

You underestimate the power of the Dark Side.

DARTH VADER

It is quite easy for us who live in a Western society to ignore the reality of a spiritual realm. For many generations we have been perfectly comfortable accepting a world that consists only of what is natural and physical—things we can see and explain. The spiritual world has become the stuff of make believe—nothing more than fairy tales and sci-fi.

However, a much broader acceptance of the spiritual realm has now worked its way into mainstream Western society. Eastern mysticism and vague personal spirituality have become popular and acceptable in the past few years, but rarely do you hear anyone acknowledging the possibility that this spirituality could be negative or dangerous. Even within the church, there exists a growing segment that accepts the existence of God while simultaneously rejecting the existence of Satan.

Once you reject the reality of an adversary who is fighting against all that is good, you lose the ability to explain the undeniable evil in this world. One of the main arguments atheists use to justify their disbelief of God is the inability to reconcile evil with a God who is supposed to be good and loving. They ask questions such as "If God is so good, why does He allow so much suffering to exist in this world?" and "Why do bad things happen to good people?" If you ignore the reality of spiritual conflict, which, by the very nature of being a battle, requires two opposing forces, many such issues arise. Once you acknowledge the truth of Satan being active in the world today, though, it suddenly shines a lot of light on those questions.

Not long ago in Connecticut, a gunman walked into an elementary school and fired at anyone he could, regardless of age. Twenty children and six adults were murdered. There have since been lengthy discussions about how a man could reach such a point of depravity, and the general consensus is mental illness. Is it really so much easier to accept the idea of a chemical imbalance in someone's brain telling him to murder innocent children than to accept the idea of an intelligent and nefarious being actively deceiving him? To me this makes no sense. In other parts of the world, though, there would be little doubt that someone who committed an atrocity like this was under the influence of an evil spirit.

I still feel a bit crazy mentioning the reality of the spiritual world to people. There's something about the idea of Satan whispering ideas into your ear that brings to mind images of a tiny man in red tights standing on your shoulder telling you to drop an anvil on an unsuspecting rabbit. I believe this is all by Satan's design, though. As long as he can convince people he doesn't exist, he can continue to deceive them without ever being questioned. What if there are subtle whispers in your mind trying to convince you that an image on a website will meet some need in your life (or condemning you by telling you how shameful and wretched you are for looking at those images). Aren't you willing to consider whether these whispers might be coming from a source outside of you? If not, what options are you left with? You are left to believe that these thoughts must be your own. You may even start to believe them to be true. It's a subtle yet crafty plan the devil has used for millennia, which has resulted in immense pain and bondage for those who remain unaware of it.

Satan's Only Weapon is the Lie

Satan no longer has any power over you. None. When Christ died on the cross, He defeated sin and death once and for all. Therefore, if you have placed your hope in Him, you have also been freed from the power of sin and death:

> Because you belong to him, the power of the life-giving Spirit has freed you from the power of sin that leads to death (Romans 8:2).

But if we truly are dead to sin (and we are), why does it still feel like we are controlled by sin? It's because Satan is a liar, and he has deceived you into believing that you are still under sin's curse. He knows he has no power over you anymore, so he must rely on his only remaining weapon to hurt you—deception. No, he can't make you a slave to sin anymore, but he will still take every opportunity to try and convince you that you still are.

He knows he's already lost the battle, but that doesn't mean he's going away without a fight. This is why it is crucial to consider where any thought or belief is actually coming from, as not all thoughts come from your own mind, or from God. Many thoughts and accusations come from evil sources with the sole purpose of leading you away from the truth:

> The Spirit makes it clear that as time goes on, some are going to give up on the faith and chase after demonic illusions put forth by professional liars. These liars have lied so well and for so long that they've lost their capacity for truth (1 Timothy 4:1–2 MSG).

The Danger of Believing Lies

Just because a lie isn't true doesn't mean it won't cause damage. Imagine if a national news anchor made a false report about a foreign country firing nuclear missiles toward multiple cities in the United States and told us that the first impacts would hit within the hour, which means evacuation is not possible. There would be mass panic and hysteria, regardless of whether the story was true or not.

Or, what if a doctor wrongly diagnosed you with a terminal disease and gave you only a month to live? Would it change the way you lived your life even though there was no truth to the diagnosis? What if you decided you were going to seek the best treatment you could find and fight the disease with reckless abandon? You could research all the medical journals, seek out the most knowledgeable doctors, attempt cutting-edge treatments, and even take the most potent medications available. But would any of these things help you? Of course not! The issue was never how much resolve you had to fight the disease or whether you had enough knowledge about it. The issue is the fact that the disease is not real. You cannot fix a problem that doesn't exist. In fact, by trying to fix the nonexistent disease, you may even be doing yourself more harm. There is no point in trying to change a behavior when all that needs to change is the belief.

Satan continues to mess with us in much the same way. He will diagnose you as wretched and terrible—completely unworthy to come before God unless you clean yourself up first. He will convince you that no one else is anywhere near as bad as you are. He will tempt you to accept rotten and poisonous sin by lying to you about how delicious and satisfying it will be. Furthermore, if you do give in to his temptations, he will respond by dumping shame, guilt, and condemnation upon you for being so weak. None of these things are true about you of course, but they can still be very damaging if you believe them to be true.

The Cause of Spiritual Bondage

The real reason so many of us remain in bondage to our sin is not because we are still slaves to it; it's because we have come to believe certain lies about ourselves—or about God. Yes, your addiction feels real and present. I am in no way saying that your bondage is a lie. But the nature and source of your bondage may be very different from what you have believed so far.

Before we go on, it's important to recognize that *bondage* and *possession* are not the same thing. Demonic forces will never be able to *possess* you. They will never be strong enough to overcome the protection of the Holy Spirit within you and gain control your life.[1] There is a very real possibility,

1 1 John 4:4.

however, that you might invite them to establish strongholds (bondage) within you if you take your eyes off the truth. Are you possessed at that point? No, but you are very much influenced.

The account of the Trojan horse is a great illustration for how these strongholds are created within us. The Greek army knew there was no way they could penetrate the walls of the city of Troy by sheer force or military might, so they devised a plan to fool the Trojans and slip past their defenses. A small company of men hid inside a giant wooden horse while the rest of the army retreated back into the woods, feigning defeat. The Trojans believed they had won the war and brought the horse inside their walls as a trophy to commemorate their victory.

Now that the Trojans believed the threat of war was over, they let their guard down and started to party. But that very night, while they slept off their hangovers, the Greeks snuck out of the horse and unlocked the gates for the rest of their army to enter. They made quick work of the unsuspecting Trojans. The Trojans didn't lose the battle because they were the weaker army; they lost the battle because they allowed the enemy to penetrate their defenses through deception.

In the same way, Satan will try to convince you that something other than God (sin) will bring you happiness or meet some need in your life. He will attempt to trick you into opening the door for his army to establish an enemy camp within you. This is why it is so important for you to be aware of his deceitful methods for gaining access to your life.

Becoming One...with Many

There appears to be an additional element of spiritual bondage that comes with sexual sins:

> There is a sense in which sexual sins are different from all others. In sexual sin we violate the sacredness of our own bodies, these bodies that were made for God-given and God-modeled love, for "becoming one" with another (1 Corinthians 6:18 MSG).

Each time you engage in sexual activity with a woman, your souls unite and you "become one," which means you connect with each other spiritually. God's plan has always been for this to be an integral part of marriage, resulting in a beautiful unity between the husband and wife. This is why you likely still feel a strong connection to each of your past sexual partners, even if you have not seen them in years.

Each time this bond is created between two people outside of marriage, though, it opens the door for the devil to create another stronghold, tightening the chains of bondage around both partners.

Breaking the Chains of Spiritual Bondage in Your Life[2]

The moment you put your faith in Christ, you received all the power and authority you need for the strongholds in your life to be broken. The only step required of you is to stop fighting on your own and trust God to set you free using His power.

One way to do this is by praying something along these lines:

Father, I am choosing to trust in your power alone to set me free from any spiritual bondage in my life. Please bring to my mind anything that has allowed the devil to set up a stronghold within me.

I suggest having a notepad handy to write down everything the Lord brings to mind. There may be obvious things, such as sexual sins, drug use, or participation in cultic practices. There will likely be some more subtle things as well, such as certain movies you have watched, or even things that were done to you against your will. Odds are good that you will even have some stuff come to mind that seems trivial and you may be tempted to ignore it. Please don't. Trust the Holy Spirit and ignore the temptation to brush over these "little" things.

If you're anything like me, you'll end up with a substantial list. Once you feel that your list is complete, bring each item before the Lord with the following prayer:

2 I owe credit for many of the concepts in this section to Neil Anderson's book *The Bondage Breaker*. As I mentioned in my story, this book was instrumental in my own journey to freedom. I strongly encourage you to pick up a copy for yourself, as it will give you a much deeper understanding of the concepts I am sharing here. Seriously, read *The Bondage Breaker*.

Lord, I bring ____________ under the healing power of the cross. I confess this act to you as sin and renounce my participation in it. I thank you for the forgiveness and cleansing that you have promised me in your Word. I ask you to break any spiritual, emotional, or physical stronghold the devil has established within me as a result. I trust that your blood has the power to set me free from all bondage. Thank you, Jesus.

Pray this for each item on your list, and choose to believe that Christ really can set you free. Satan will be trying every trick in his book to distract you from this prayer because he knows better than anyone that it's his kryptonite. So there's a good chance your skepticism is coming directly from him. Don't believe the lie, though. Pray it until you believe it.

Freedom from Nightmares

The freedom I experienced from pornography after reaching out to God through this prayer was not the only blessing. Within a few weeks I realized my frequent nightmares and visions were gone as well. Before that moment, I would have intense and frightening dreams of being chased or pursued by something evil, causing me to wake up with my heart racing, full of fear and anxiety. What really worried me, though, were the nights when I would wake up and see giant spiders, bats, or shadows on the ceiling about to drop down on me. I would jump out of bed quickly to turn on the light—which I am sure freaked out my wife—but nothing was there once the light was on. The amazing thing is, I have not had a single nightmare after asking God to release me from the spiritual bondage in my life.

I was extremely skeptical the first time I prayed a prayer like this, but God used it to set me free. When I asked Him to bring to mind all of the areas where I had allowed Satan to gain a foothold in my life, He brought to mind each woman I had slept with outside of marriage, countless times of viewing pornography, my past experiences with drugs, and even things such as playing with a Ouija board in middle school. No matter what popped into my head, though, I trusted that it was God bringing it to my mind to be dealt with, and handed it all over to Him. And as you read in my story, the chains of my addiction were broken instantly.

I wish I could say that this prayer is a one-and-done deal, but it's not. God can definitely set you free in a moment, but you must continue to walk closely with Him in order to remain free. The reality is, your life here on Earth will always be a spiritual battle. There are evil forces that want nothing more than to destroy you, and they will stop at nothing to rob you of your newfound freedom. Thankfully, God never intended for you to fight this battle alone, and He has given you a solution:

> Put on every piece of God's armor so you will be able to resist the enemy in the time of evil. Then after the battle you will still be standing firm (Ephesians 6:13).

Preparing for the Continual Battle

When you put on God's armor, you place yourself under His protection. Yes, you are still responsible to resist the temptation, but it's His armor that will give you the power to do so.

But what exactly is the armor of God? Paul goes on to explain this concept further:

> Stand your ground, putting on the belt of truth and the body armor of God's righteousness. For shoes, put on the peace that comes from the Good News so that you will be fully prepared. In addition to all of these, hold up the shield of faith to stop the fiery arrows of the devil. Put on salvation as your helmet, and take the sword of the Spirit, which is the word of God. Pray in the Spirit at all times and on every occasion. Stay alert and be persistent in your prayers for all believers everywhere (Ephesians 6:14–18).

We are told that the very first thing we need to put on is the belt of truth. In other words, it is essential that seeking the truth of God's Word is your first step in any battle. You must ask God to show you the truth behind the battle you are fighting or you risk wasting time fighting the wrong battle. Ask Him if this temptation you are currently facing is merely a symptom of something deeper? Ask if you're feeling a draw to pornography because you are horny, or because you truly desire something else? What is the *real* battle? It's God's truth that will strengthen and guide you as you remain in this world and experience temptations.[3] Or to put it another way, when you are tempted to look at pornography, only the belt of truth will keep your pants up.[4]

The next step is to put on the body armor of God's righteousness. Satan will try to convince you that you are not righteous because you are still dealing with temptation. He will try to discredit you because you are not perfect. But remember, God declares you to be righteous, so you are righteous indeed. By trusting in His free gift of His righteousness rather than your own attempts at generating righteousness, you remain dependent on Him to keep you safe in the battle.

And what about the "Good News Shoes"? I always found them to be a bit of an enigma until I really started to experience God's peace in my life. I now like to think of them more like athletic shoes, allowing me to have ninja-like agility as I sneak across enemy lines to share the good news of Christ with those who are still in captivity. After all, once you experience the peace and freedom that comes from Christ's work in your life, you won't be able to hold back your desire to share this good news with others who are still in captivity. You will want to keep your shoes on so you are always ready when the moment arises.

By this point in your life, you are undoubtedly aware of the fiery arrows of accusation the devil launches at you. Thankfully, we are given a powerful tool—the shield of faith—to protect us from them. By choosing to trust that everything God says about us is true, we can recognize and resist these false accusations from the devil. He may call you a failure or an addict, or send some other flaming arrow of accusation, but it will bounce off your shield when your faith is placed on God's description of you—that you are no longer a sinner, but a saint.

---

3 John 17:15–17.

4 And now you know why we are called Belt of Truth Ministries (www.beltoftruth.com).

The helmet of salvation is what protects your mind and your thoughts. When you live your life knowing you will spend eternity with Christ, Satan's attempts to distract you become much less interesting. The things of this world won't seem like much in comparison to the riches you know you have in Christ. Focusing on your eternal salvation puts the things of this world into a right perspective.

It's important to understand that our main focus in spiritual warfare is never to fight Satan, but to resist him. This is why we are called to put on the armor of God as a defensive measure. We are not given an offensive arsenal with which to seek out battles on our own. There will be times when we do need to fight back, though, which is why we are told to pick up the sword of the Spirit—the Word of God—as our weapon of choice. When the attacks are severe and intense, nothing will strike down the enemy like Scripture. We are shown a powerful example of this in Jesus' temptation by the devil in the wilderness.[5] Every temptation Satan threw at Him, He countered by quoting Scripture and exposing the lie with truth. Satan had no answers and was forced to flee. The Word of God is a powerful weapon against his lies.

Finally, now that you have put on your armor for battle and picked up your sword, there still remains one very important step—you must pray. God wants to help you in this fight, but He tends to wait until you ask Him. So ask Him to reveal to you anything you are believing that is a lie and to show you the truth. Ask Him to protect you from all sources of temptation and give you the strength to resist them. He wants to come beside you, equip you, and rescue you—this is what He has promised in His Word:

> The temptations in your life are no different from what others experience. And God is faithful. He will not allow the temptation to be more than you can stand. When you are tempted, he will show you a way out so that you can endure (1 Corinthians 10:13).

---

5 Matthew 4:1–11.

You have a very real, and very dangerous, adversary. But the good news is you have an even greater Advocate—Jesus.[6] And because of the work He did on the cross, Satan has been defeated and no longer has any power over you:

> He canceled the record of the charges against us and took it away by nailing it to the cross. In this way, he disarmed the spiritual rulers and authorities. He shamed them publicly by his victory over them on the cross (Colossians 2:14–15).

The war for your soul is over—you have been sealed with Christ in heaven. Jesus has won the battle, and there is nothing that can ever change that.

And that, my friend, is the Truth.

---

6 1 John 2:1–2.

LIE #1

My Pornography Addiction Defines Who I Am

I was walking in the park and this guy waved at me. Then he said, "I'm sorry, I thought you were someone else." I said, "I am."

DEMETRI MARTIN

Who are you?

If you're anything like most people, especially men, your first response to that question is probably your job title. After that, you may list off your age, how many kids you have, or perhaps even your hobbies. If I had been asked that question a few years back, I would have answered, "I am a graphic designer." This is true, but it's not really who I am—it's just what I do to pay the bills. I might also have told you that I am a dad to the coolest (and cutest) girl in the world, that I like being in the mountains, and that I love bacon almost as much as I love air. Here's the deal, though—these things may *describe* me, but they do not *define* me. In order to figure out what defines you—your true identity—you need to understand who your Creator says you are. After all, He's the One who made you, so He is the only one with the authority to give you an identity.

TRUTH: Only God can define who you are.

If you don't understand who God says you are, you are left to fill your identity void on your own. Anywhere you look outside of Him will result in a false identity, because your true identity is not something you can create or achieve—it can only be received.

Satan will try to exploit your identity void in a myriad of ways in order to wreak havoc in your life. One of the most prolific ways he does this is by convincing you that your identity is defined by your sin—or by the sins of others against you. How many times have you thought, *I am a terrible sinner,* or placed labels on yourself such as *stupid, worthless, dirty, failure,* and so on? Once you look to the Bible and see the truth about what God says about you, you will see that none of these labels are true about you. They are all false identities.

Common False Identities

Not all false identities are based on "bad things." In fact, it's quite common for men to seek to find their identity in things most people would consider to be good. The problem with this approach, though, is these "good things" tend to become "god things," because we allow them to replace God as the most important part of our lives.

In order to see this more clearly, let's take a look at a few of the more common false identities men tend to latch onto.

Social Groups

I had no idea who I was in middle school, so I kept trying on new identities to see if any of them would bring me lasting fulfillment. And like most teenagers, I believed that fulfillment would come once I discovered an identity that granted me acceptance into the right social group.

I tried out life as the funny kid, desiring to be loved and accepted for my wit and humor. When that didn't work, I tried to define myself as a Rollerblader, hoping that the athletic adrenaline junkie crowd would think I was cool. I actually wore my kneepads and wrist guards all day at school so everyone could see how hardcore I was (it was the '90s—cut me some slack).

Nothing ever fit quite right, so I started experimenting with shadier identities—rebel, smoker, stoner, raver, and on down the line. Every time

I tried on a new identity, I would jump into the new culture with reckless abandon in an attempt to gain answers to who I truly was. This pursuit led me into all kinds of negative behaviors, like shoplifting, drug use, and heavy partying. Ironically, I continued to stay involved with my church youth group this entire time, yet I never thought to look at who God said I was. I kept looking to my circle of friends to define me.

We really aren't that different as adults, are we? We may have become smarter about navigating social circles since we were in high school, but the underlying search for an identity still continues. Many of us are still searching for our identities in the sports team we root for, the political party we support, or other social circles we are proud to be a part of.

For example, are some Yankee fans so passionately opposed to Red Sox fans because they have placed their identity in being a Yankee, and to root against the Yankees is to root against them as a person? Likewise, if your identity is in a political party and someone votes for the opposing party, it feels like they are voting against you personally. Every time they state an opinion your party disagrees with, you take it as an assault on your own character.

When you allow your social circles to define who you are, you end up seeking fulfillment and happiness from a group of people and the circumstances that surround them. When things are going well, you are happy. When people agree with you and accept you, life seems wonderful. But what happens when things change for the worse, as they inevitably will? This is why it's so important to find your identity in something—or more specifically, Someone—who will never change.

Hobbies

I could write an entire book outlining all the ways I've attempted to find my identity through hobbies, but there is one that stands above the rest—being a mountain man. Here's a segment I wrote for an outdoor podcast explaining what I mean in a little more detail:

> Once I got a taste of mountain climbing I was hooked. Our shared hobby of hiking as a couple had mutated into a singular passion that my wife didn't share. She would have been more

> than willing to go for a hike with me along a beautiful river, or even an overnight backpacking trip to a majestic mountain lake, but I had become obsessed with climbing and, over time, allowed the "We" trips to all become "Me" trips. I'd be gone for hours on training runs or hauling my pack up the local hill multiple times a week. In the rare event that I was home physically, I was in the mountains mentally. The more I pursued climbing, the less I pursued my wife. I started to see her as a hurdle in my climbing quest. I stopped asking her if I could leave for the weekend and started telling her that I would be gone. I couldn't see it at the time, but I had chosen the mountains over her.[1]

I had allowed mountain climbing to become my false identity. I had found something I was good at, and it seemed to impress others. I could strike up a conversation with people and once they found out I was a climber they were suddenly more interested in talking with me. People knew me as the guy who climbs mountains, which made me feel rugged, macho, and manly. As Dr. Phil might say, it stoked my male ego.

But hobbies can never define you on the deepest level or show you who you truly are. You can keep climbing taller mountains, master your golf swing, or take bigger and bigger risks in the stock market hoping that it will finally meet some unknown need in your life, but you will always need to come back for more when the satisfaction inevitably wears off. Sure, hobbies are great and highly fulfilling, but if you are honest with yourself, you probably sense that no matter how much time and effort you devote to them, you will always crave just a little bit more. Your hobby may be something you do, something you enjoy, but if you allow it to become who you are—your false identity—it will fail you.

Romantic Relationships

Perhaps one of the more damaging tricks Satan plays on men is to convince them to look to romantic relationships to find their identity. This is

1 You can listen to the podcast at http://dirtbagdiaries.com/the-shorts-dream-interrupted.

one reason why men are so easily drawn to porn—because it can temporarily make them feel as if they've found the missing piece of their soul they've been searching for. But no woman, regardless of whether she is flesh and blood or pixels on a screen, can ever give a man his true identity.

I bought into this lie big time. I sought my identity through romantic relationships for the majority of my postpubescent life, which explains why most of those relationships were long-term but *always* ended in disaster.

I can now see that the pattern was quite predictable. I would meet a girl who was interested in me and quickly become captivated by her. I'd adjust my entire life to orbit around her—spending as much time with her as I could—often at the expense of all other relationships. Her friends became my friends. Her interests became my interests. We would quickly become sexually active, which made me feel validation as a man. All of this fed into me establishing my identity—and seeking my fulfillment—in being "So-and-so's guy."

Over time, though, the identity I was seeking would never satisfy because it wasn't the true answer to who I was. The feeling that something was missing in the relationship would become stronger and stronger, and I would begin to feel a desire to look elsewhere for answers. Once I reached this point, the girl would inevitably sense me disconnecting from her. She would begin to feel like she wasn't good enough for me anymore but didn't know why. Once this began to happen, it was only a matter of time before we would start drifting apart.

Eventually, I would meet some new girl and start to feel like she might be the answer. My current girlfriend wouldn't seem to be meeting my need for fulfillment in life, so perhaps this new girl, complete with all the passions that come with a new relationship, would be what I was missing. So I would break up with my current girlfriend, move on to the new one, and the cycle would repeat itself.

This same pattern defined my marriage as well. By the time I started to feel that my wife was no longer satisfying my need for an identity, she had already sensed my distance and taken personal responsibility for it as if it were her fault. Her self-esteem plummeted as she became more and more confused about what was happening to us. My expectations of her validating me and providing me with an identity had put her in an impossible position. It was wreaking havoc on her and on our marriage. It breaks my heart to look back at this now because I see how much pain I could have saved my wife, as well as my previous girlfriends, if I had recognized this pattern earlier.

I can't tell you how many couples I have seen divorce for no better reason than "we just don't get along anymore" or "irreconcilable differences." But what causes two people who deeply love each other to grow apart and eventually give up? What causes a couple to move from craving each other's company every chance they get to fighting intensely about which brand of coffee to buy? Are these fights actually the outpouring of frustration resulting from your spouse not meeting your need for validation—a need she was never designed to meet in the first place? Are you placing unspoken and impossible expectations upon her and setting her up for inevitable failure? As long as you look to someone other than God to provide your identity, she will fail you, and it will cause pain for everyone involved.

The moment any one of my false identities began to fail me, I would attempt to fix it by focusing all of my time and energy on it, often resulting in great neglect of other areas of my life. After all, if my identity truly did come from these things, what would happen if any of them failed? I couldn't bear to find out. What I didn't realize, though, was these false identities were actually distracting me from recognizing that my identity could only come from Christ alone.

Who God Says You Are

As far as God is concerned, there are only two possible identities for every man, woman, and child alive today. You are either "in Adam," or you are "in Christ." You must be one or the other, and you cannot be both. The most important thing to understand in regards to your identity—and ultimately in your battle against temptation—is which camp you belong to.

You are No Longer "in Adam"

The moment Adam chose to turn away from God and share the fruit with his wife, the cancer of sin entered into the human race and changed the default identity of everyone.[2] Since that day, every one of us have been born physically alive but spiritually dead:

> When Adam sinned, sin entered the world. Adam's sin brought death, so death spread to everyone, for everyone sinned (Romans 5:12).

Our identity at birth is now "in Adam," which means we are all born with a sin nature.

If you are a parent, it shouldn't be too hard to understand this. Unless your name is Mary, your sweet little kiddo didn't need to be taught how to sin. It's in their nature from day one to be selfish, to lie to you, to yell "NO!" when asked to do something they don't want to do. Did you ever sit down and have a conversation with junior discussing the benefits of dishonesty and how manipulation can be used for his gain? Of course not. Any child knows these things because they are born with a sin nature.

As long as your identity is still "in Adam," you are separated from God because of this sin nature within you. You are spiritually dead. If this is your reality, the lie of this chapter is unfortunately true for you—your sin really does define you. You can do all sorts of good things here on earth, but ultimately none of them will matter in eternity because they will be done for your own benefit and not for God's glory. You are also forced to live your life, fight your temptations, and manage your pain using your own power. You are on your own. This does not mean God is not actively pursuing you while you remain "in Adam" (He certainly is), but ultimately you will need to reach out to Him and accept His help.

Don't be discouraged by this, though. If you are reading this book, there's a good chance your identity is no longer "in Adam." Why? Because the moment you placed your hope and trust in Jesus, your identity switched to "in Christ," and the separation no longer describes you! Satan will still try to convince you that even though you have placed your hope in Jesus (in Christ), you are still defined by your sin (in Adam). But remember, you are either "in Adam" or "in Christ." It's fully one or fully the other. You cannot be both.

---

2 See Genesis 3.

You are "in Christ"

Just as everyone is born "in Adam," everyone is also given the opportunity to be born again "in Christ." The moment you place your hope and trust in Jesus to rescue you and set you free from your sinful nature, you are reborn with a new nature—a new identity. Your identity is now "in Christ."

Chances are, you have a pretty good understanding that being "in Christ" means you are now reconciled to God. Even if you haven't spent much time in church, you're probably still familiar with John 3:16:

> God loved the world so much that he gave his one and only Son, so that everyone who believes *in him* will not perish but have eternal life (John 3:16),

When we believe in Christ, we receive eternal life in heaven with God. Most churches do a wonderful job of preaching this central truth of salvation. What is sometimes missed, though, is the truth that this life "in Christ" is available to us right now! If we understand the gospel as merely the promise of eternal life after death, we remain stuck trying to live life here on earth in our own power—living as if we are still "in Adam." We miss the reality that God has promised us His life (and all the benefits that come with it) today. It begins the moment our identity changes from "in Adam" to "in Christ."

Let's take a look at what Jesus teaches us about what it means to be in Him:

> Yes, I am the vine; you are the branches. Those who remain *in me*, and I *in them*, will produce much fruit. For apart from me you can do nothing (John 15:5).

This verse is a great positional statement showing us what happens when we live with an understanding that our true identity is in Christ: We will produce much fruit. We will receive His power in us to live the life He has for us. We will see all the fruits of the Spirit—love, joy, peace, patience, kindness, goodness, faithfulness, gentleness, and self-control flow from our lives.[3]

But what happens if we don't understand that we are "in Christ"? We

3 Galatians 5:22–23.

will live our lives as if we are a disconnected branch and will quickly become discouraged by our inability to produce fruit by ourselves.

And what about those who believe they are doing just fine and don't see their need to be connected to Christ—those who choose to remain "in Adam"? No matter how hard they try, they will never bear fruit. They will be like a branch cut off from the vine left to wither and die on the ground. For apart from Christ, they can do nothing.

How many of you, like me, read this verse a hundred times thinking, *I don't see much fruit in my life...does this mean I'm not really connected to Christ?* Thoughts such as those are precisely what come when you do not realize that, once your identity is "in Christ," it will never revert to "in Adam." As long as you are questioning the security of your identity in Christ, you will live as if you are still partially "in Adam." You will attempt to produce fruit on your own in order to confirm your own salvation. But it will never work, because you can only produce fruit if you are living out of your true identity in Christ. That's because fruit isn't the *proof* of being in Christ; it is the *product* of being in Christ.

Perhaps this will be easier to understand if we back up a few verses and see what else Jesus says in this passage:

> You have already been pruned and purified by the message I have given you. Remain in me, and I will remain in you. For a branch cannot produce fruit if it is severed from the vine, and you cannot be fruitful unless you remain in me (John 15:2–4).

Did you catch that? You have *already* been pruned and purified through Jesus. The reason you may be experiencing a season of unfruitfulness is not because you were cut off or never attached, it is because you have believed the lie that you are not permanently attached to Christ. You are believing that something, usually sin, has separated you from Him. Simply put, you were not *remaining* in Him.

Furthermore, you may have been striving to produce fruit in your own power in an attempt to prove that you really were in Him. But the key to living in your true identity isn't to try to become who you think God wants you to be; it's to trust that you already are who God says you are. If you trust that Christ is really in you, and you really are in Christ, fruit will flow naturally. Like most truths in Scripture, though, you must choose to believe this first in order fully experience it.

Understanding Who You are in Christ

We could look at a hundred verses on what it means to be in Christ, and every one is amazing. I encourage you to do your own Bible study on the phrases "in Christ" and "in Him," to see for yourself. You may even want to substitute your own name to make them more personal. For example, if we only look at a few such verses from Ephesians we see the following:

- [*Your name*] is chosen by God in Christ to be holy and without fault (1:4).
- [*Your name*'s] purpose in Christ is to bring praise and glory to God (1:12).
- By believing in Christ, [*your name*] is identified as God's own and has received the Holy Spirit (1:13).
- [*Your name*] has been created anew in Christ to do the good things prepared for him by God (2:10).
- [*Your name*] is joined together with all other believers in Him and is now a temple for the Lord (2:21).
- [*Your name*] has endless treasures available to him in Christ (3:8).
- Because of Christ and our faith in him, [*your name*] can now come boldly and confidently into God's presence (3:12).
- Then Christ will make his home in [*your name*'s] heart as [*your name*] trusts in him. [*Your name*'s] roots will grow down into God's love and keep [*your name*] strong (3:17).

Throughout Scripture you will find these verses describing your true identity in Christ. Take the time to study this concept and dig deeper. Believe these verses are true about you because *all* Scripture is true—whether it feels like it is or not. This may be one of the most life-changing studies you ever do.[4]

You are No Longer a Sinner, You are a Saint

Would you believe me if I told you anyone who is in Christ is no longer a sinner? What if God told you it was true? The truth is, He has told you just that:

> You also should consider yourselves to be dead to the power of sin and alive to God through Christ Jesus (Romans 6:11).

When Christ took all of your sin upon Himself on the cross, He destroyed its power over you. Because of this, your previous identity of "sinner" died along with Christ:

> My old self [sinner] has been crucified with Christ. It is no longer I who live, but Christ lives in me. So I live in this earthly body by trusting in the Son of God, who loved me and gave himself for me (Galatians 2:20).

Now that the power of sin over me has been broken, I can trust that Christ living within me will empower me to live the life He has called me to. But not only that, I can also trust Him when He says that I am truly dead to sin. Which means I am no longer a sinner—I am a saint!

Saint Stephen?

Before everyone gets all puckered up about the word "saint," it might be a good idea to pause and take a look at the biblical definition.

Many of us will hear the word "saint" and immediately think of the way it is commonly used within certain religious systems. But this act of bestowing the label of "sainthood" on an individual by a religious organization simply isn't found in the Bible.

When we look to the Bible to define "saint," we see the term being used to

4 Every Thursday, I share a new "in Christ" verse on my blog at www.beltoftruth.com. If you subscribe, they will come straight to your inbox every week and can serve as excellent reminders of who you are in Christ.

describe *everyone* who is in Christ. Paul begins multiple letters by addressing them to the "saints." Some translations use the phrase "God's holy people," which is the same idea. Here's the deal: These letters were written to the *entire* body of believers within each city—even the guy sitting in the back row who only trusted in Christ yesterday, still smokes, and continues to cuss like a sailor. It's not just a label for the "varsity" believers who have achieved some special status.

According to the biblical definition, everyone who is in Christ, regardless of how far along they are on their journey toward sanctification, becomes a saint the moment they trust in Jesus. Being a saint has nothing to do with how good you are. It's the biblical identity of everyone who is in Christ.

In the same way that you cannot be both "in Adam" and "in Christ," you cannot be both a saint and a sinner. You are one or the other. In order to reconcile this with what feels like a very different reality—we all still sin—we need to look at it a bit deeper.

First, what is the definition of a sinner? One who sins, right? Nope. A sinner is one who can do nothing *but* sin. See the difference? If you are still separated from Christ, everything you do, no matter how noble or good it is, is done *apart* from Him. And anything done apart from Christ is sin. If you are in Him, though, you now have the ability to do good things "in Christ"—things that are *not* sin. Likewise, a saint is not someone who never sins, but someone who doesn't *have to* sin. Sin has lost its power over you. You are not a sinner who has been saved, but a saint who sometimes gives in to sin.

We see this being played out with Paul as he shares his own continuing struggle with sin:

> ...I want to do what is right, but I can't. I want to do what is good, but I don't. I don't want to do what is wrong, but I do it anyway. But if I do what I don't want to do, I am not really the one doing wrong; it is sin living in me that does it.
>
> I have discovered this principle of life—that when I want to do what is right, I inevitably do what is wrong. I love God's

> law with all my heart. But there is another power within me that is at war with my mind. This power makes me a slave to the sin that is still within me (Romans 7:18–23).

Sounds familiar, right? This same battle played out in my mind every time I gave in to porn. *Why do I keep doing this if I'm supposedly dead to sin?* Paul can't really be "dead to sin" if he's writing this, can he? Well, let's look closer. Paul clearly states in this passage that he loves God's law with all his heart. We also know he is a follower of Christ at this point by reading the rest of the letter, so it's clear that he is "in Christ." Therefore, he must also be dead to sin. But why does he still struggle? The key to understanding this seeming contradiction is to notice a few easily overlooked phrases.

First: "I am not the one doing wrong; it is sin living in me that does it." Did you catch that? *Sin* is doing these actions within Paul. Not Paul. Paul is a saint—dead to sin and alive to Christ. This sin does not define him, but it still influences him. It has no ability to change his standing in Christ, but it can still wreak havoc in his life.

This sin within us is commonly referred to as "the flesh" throughout the New Testament. The flesh is not us; it is a false self—a lie. At the end of our life here on Earth, it will die, but the real you will continue to exist. That is why Paul says it is not really he who is sinning but the flesh within him. His true identity—who he really is—is completely separate from this sin within him. It does not define him.

Second: "There is another power within me that is at war with my mind. This power makes me a slave to the sin that is still within me." Something else is inside of Paul. Something that is *not* Paul. The power he is referring to here is the devil and all of his minions, who are constantly trying to convince you that your sin *does* define you. They are trying to get you to lose sight of the reality that you are dead to sin. These powers are waging a war within Paul's mind (and our minds as well) by whispering lies and accusations in an attempt to lure him back into the bondage of sin.

As one who is "in Christ," though, you are no longer a slave to sin. But if you believe Satan's lie that you still are a slave, you will continue to live as if his accusation is true. As long as you still believe your identity is "sinner," you will believe that you have no choice but to give in to sin whenever temptation comes. If, however, you believe that you are a saint, you will trust the Word of God when it says that sin is no longer your master. And once you chose to trust the Word, you can begin to live in the truth it declares.

You are a Child of God

You know what's absolutely amazing? The God of the universe, Creator of Earth, the One who holds everything together, has adopted *you* as His child. But don't just take my word for it:

> To all who believed him and accepted him, he gave the right to become children of God (John 1:12).
>
> All who are led by the Spirit of God are children of God (Romans 8:14).
>
> You are all children of God through faith in Christ Jesus (Galatians 3:26).

Think about that for a second and just try to comprehend what it means. If you're a parent, consider how much you love your kids. As much as you love them, though, it's with an imperfect, human love. God loves you even more than you love your kids, because He loves you with His holy, unconditional, and righteous God-love.

Jesus tells us an amazing story of God the Father's love in the parable of the lost son.[5] In the story, a rebellious son demands his inheritance from his father immediately. Culturally, this was the same as telling his father, "You're dead to me now." But rather than yelling at his son or punishing him, the father gives his son the money, lets him leave, and waits in anticipation for his return. Every day the father looks off into the distance, hoping to see his son returning. When the son finally does return, the father doesn't even give his boy a chance to grovel. He runs to him with open arms and tackle-hugs him at full speed! No matter how much

5 Traditionally, the "prodigal son." Luke 15:11–32.

the boy rejected or disobeyed His dad, there was nothing he could have done to make his father stop loving him.

Do you realize this is actually a story about God's love for you? No matter how much you've messed up, He will always be standing there with His arms wide open—just like the father in the story—waiting for you to come home to Him. It doesn't matter what you've done or where you've been. None of it will make any difference in how much He loves you.

I didn't understand the depth of a love like this until my daughter was born. I can say without a doubt that there is nothing my girl could ever do to make me stop loving her. No matter how many times she hits me as a toddler, yells at me as a teenager, or disowns me as an adult, I will always be there waiting for her with open arms. I simply cannot fathom living my life apart from my favorite little girl no matter what she does. Honestly. I'm even getting a bit choked up now just typing these words and thinking about how much I love her. But as much as she means to me as my daughter, you mean even more to God as His adopted son.

What if "Father" is a Difficult Word?

I was blessed with an earthly dad who made it easy for me to embrace this idea of God as my Father, but I know that a lot of fathers have made this a very difficult concept to grasp. For those of you with angry, abusive, absent, or nonexistent fathers—I am so sorry you had to experience that pain. I wish I had an easy answer or solution for the suffering you experienced, but there is none. Please consider looking to God as your heavenly Father, though, understanding that He is a good Father and loves you with a perfect love.

As your heavenly Father, God wants to heal you from the pain of your past, not add to it.

You Have Full Access to God

As a child of God, you have full access to God whenever you want. You can come before God and ask Him to help you with your struggles, give you His strength to make it through a difficult circumstance, or give you His wisdom in a specific situation. You can come before Him and ask Him *anything*, because you have *full* access:

> All of us can come to the Father through the same Holy Spirit because of what Christ has done for us (Ephesians 2:18).

Not only that, the Father actually *wants* us to come before Him with our needs and desires. He honestly cares about whatever is on your mind:

> Give all your worries and cares to God, for he cares about you (1 Peter 5:7).

Think of it this way. How hard is it to be granted an audience with the president of the United States? Apparently, there isn't even a clear path laid out for the average citizen to meet the president. The closest I could find was a page on the presidential website allowing you to enter your name into a drawing and hopefully win an invitation to a dinner with him—but it expired two years ago. That leaves me the option of performing some amazing act of heroism that will gain me national attention, or winning the Super Bowl (I think those guys usually get a White House invitation).

But what if the president was my dad? Do the president's kids need to enter a contest to win dinner with their daddy? Nope. They can walk into the Oval Office and hang out with him pretty much whenever they want. As a child of God, you've got that same level of access to Him.

Trusting that you have Christ living inside of you, that you are a saint, and that you have full access to God as His adopted son will free you from needing to strive to measure up or attain perfection in your own power. You can rest in the knowledge that you are accepted and loved exactly as you are, because you are family. Likewise, the things of this world—success, failure, riches, fame—suddenly seem insignificant compared to your position as a child of God. This becomes the biggest thing in your life. It becomes your identity.

As one of my favorite authors, John Lynch, puts it:

He lives in you! You are in Him! How much closer do you want to be than that? Every moment of every day, fused with you, there He is. He never moves. Never covers His eyes when you sin, never puts up a newspaper, never turns His back. He's not over on the other side of your sin, waiting for you to get it together so you can finally be close. It's incredible! Don't you think? That's why they call it "Good News!"[6]

How Does This Help Me with Porn?

Imagine you are walking down a crowded street and everywhere you look you see people scowling back at you. All you hear are whispers of accusation and condemnation. Not only that, but every alley you walk by is lined with scantily clad beauties offering you illicit affairs and promising you an escape from the noise of the crowd.

Picture this scene while thinking to yourself, *I am a sinner. I'm worthless. Nobody loves me. I am a slave to my sin.*

How do you respond to the accusations? How do you respond to the sexual temptation? You will desperately want to retreat from the fear and pain caused by the verbal assaults of the crowd. When you hear the offer of love and acceptance from the alleys, it will be nearly impossible to resist its pull. You know it's sin to give in, but you already feel like a failure, so what's one more mistake going to matter? By viewing yourself as a sinner, you have resigned yourself to the fact that you will eventually give in, just as you always do.

Now, picture the same scene again, but this time, think to yourself: *I am in Christ and He is in me. I am a child of God. I am a saint. Sin has no power over me.*

Is your response any different now? I am willing to bet it is. When you view yourself this way, it becomes much easier for you to ignore the condemning voices because you know the things they are saying about you are no longer true. When you understand how much you are loved and accepted by God, you won't feel the need to seek love and acceptance from the illicit back-alley opportunities. When you understand your true identity,

6 Bill Thrall, John Lynch, and Bruce McNicol, *The Cure* (Colorado Springs: NavPress Publishing Group, 2011), 43.

it puts your eyes back onto God, His love, and what He says is true about you. It allows you to walk in His power rather than your own.

Understanding your true identity as "in Christ" will help you maintain a proper perspective. And in the same way this perspective empowers you to resist the temptations in the previous illustration, it will also empower you to resist the temptations you encounter in real life.

My Name is Stephen, and I'm a Sex Addict

I believe 12-step programs have helped countless people learn how to manage their behavior and live improved lives. For that reason, I am grateful that they exist and support them fully. That being said, I think there is one area where they are falling short of their full potential.

Standard 12-step programs will encourage you to identify yourself as an addict regardless of how long you have been sober. Yes, you may find freedom from the behavior of your addiction, but you remain shackled to your identity as an addict. As the saying goes: "Once an addict, always an addict."

Christ offers you a new identity, though. Because of His freedom, you are no longer a slave to sin, which means you no longer need to identify yourself as an addict. In fact, your addiction can't define you anymore, because it's dead. It was crucified with Christ along with the rest of your sin.

This is why the gospel message is not about learning how to merely cope with or manage your negative behaviors; it's about being reborn into a reality where your sin has been put to death once and for all.

That, my friend, is true freedom from addiction!

So let me ask you again, who are you?

Are you a sinner? Are you an addict? Not anymore, my friend!

If you have put your hope in Christ, you are a child of God! You are a saint! You are dead to sin!

Try to remind yourself of these truths every day. It's amazing the difference they will make in your life—and in your journey to freedom from pornography.

LIE #2

I am Alone in My Struggle with Pornography Addiction

Encouraging people to believe was the most important thing of all. I didn't want our make-believe to be exposed.

PATRICK STEWART

What is your biggest fear? For me personally, it's snakes. I *hate* snakes—even little, innocent, harmless garter snakes. I know they can't hurt me. I've been told they're more afraid of me than I am of them. I don't care. I despise them.

It still curls my nose hairs when I think of the woodpile we had in our backyard when I was living with my wife. As an avid gardener, she was constantly in need of more trellises and raised beds throughout the yard. I liked to swing a hammer, build stuff, and pretend to be manly—so it worked out great for both of us. One day, my dad called me and offered us an old, weathered trellis. It needed to be hauled to the dump but he figured he'd check first to see if we could use the wood. This wasn't just any trellis, though. It was over twenty feet long! So of course we jumped all over the prospect of free, pre-weathered wood. Over the years, I built a few things out of it, but the majority of it remained piled under a tarp in the back corner of our yard.

One afternoon I needed to use that tarp to line the bed of my truck. I grabbed a corner of it with one hand and threw it aside quickly so I could be ready to fight off any striking rattlers (garter snakes) with the shovel I was holding in my other hand like a spear. Once I realized there were no snakes, I relaxed, bunched up the tarp, and carried it over to my truck to spread it out. As I unfolded it, though, I saw the most terrifying thing I have seen in my entire life: Not just one, but *two* garter snakes were curled up in it. I had carried these wretched creatures in my own arms! I screamed like a little girl and did that freak-out dance where you jump and run in place at the same time while your whole body convulses in sheer terror. I'm sure I made my wife proud.

As ridiculous as this story sounds, it is completely true. Even typing it out some years later still brings a shiver to my spine. The crazy thing is, at one point in my life I actually had a fear that was even more crippling than my fear of snakes. If I were given the choice of facing this greater fear or being a stand-in for Indiana Jones in the snake temple scene, I would have asked for a whip and fedora without hesitation.

The thing I feared even more than snakes was that someday, someone might discover who I really was. I might let my guard down and allow my true self to be seen. Someone might discover that "Steve, the upstanding, churchgoing, youth-group-volunteering, hard-worker guy" was actually "Steve the porn addict." "Steve the pathological liar." "Steve the messed-up sinner."

I was convinced I was the only man sitting in church fighting this battle with pornography—or at least the only one failing at it. I desperately wanted people to like me so I tried to convince everyone I was perfect. After all, I didn't want anyone to think this whole Jesus thing wasn't working for me. I lived my life in a state of constant fear—fear of getting caught, fear of being found out, fear of being rejected if people got to know the real me. But these fears were not based on truth. They were all products of believing the lie of this chapter—that I was the only man struggling with a secret sin. Like all lies, though, they can only be defeated with an understanding of the truth. And the truth is, you are not alone in this battle.

TRUTH: You are not the only one fighting this battle, and God never intended for you to fight it alone.

The pornography industry is roughly a $5 billion a year industry. Seventy percent of men between the ages of 18 and 24 view porn at least once a month—and don't think that means anyone under the age of 18 isn't looking yet. The average age of first contact with pornography is dropping rapidly and currently sits around 11. If you need further proof that you aren't alone, 25 percent of all searches and 35 percent of all downloads are pornographic.[1] If it really is just you, that's an awful lot of time and hard-drive space for one dude. You must be pretty busy.

The truth is, pornography addiction has become an epidemic not only in the world, but within the church as well. It is estimated that more than half of all men who regularly attend church struggle with pornography on some level.[2] I'm willing to bet the number may even be higher, because survey numbers assume a certain level of honesty. There was definitely a point in my life where I wouldn't have admitted the truth about my porn usage even to an anonymous survey. But if we stick with this 50 percent estimate, it still means you are far from alone. If there are ten men sitting in your row of seats on Sunday morning, chances are good five of them are struggling just like you are. Perhaps even more surprising, your pastor isn't immune to the lure of pornography either. In fact, he may be at a greater risk, for reasons we will see later in this chapter.[3] So it's pretty clear you aren't the only guy struggling with pornography, even within your church.

I don't tell you this to justify the use of pornography. As you've undoubtedly heard your parents say, just because everyone else is doing it doesn't make it right. The reason I tell you this, is to help you recognize you are not alone. And by understanding that other men are in the same boat as you, it will become easier to believe that you are not supposed to fight this battle in isolation. You don't need to fight it alone.

Fighting the Battle on Your Own

As long as you believe the lie that you must fight this battle with

1 http://unitedfamiliesinternational.files.wordpress.com/2010/06/internet-porn.jpg.

2 ChristiaNet Inc., "ChristiaNet Poll Finds that Evangelicals are Addicted to Porn," *Marketwire*, 7 Aug. 2006. Web. 7 Dec. 2009. www.marketwire.com/press-release/Christianet-Inc-703951.html.

3 Pastors.com Survey, quoted in "Wounded Clergy," *Hope & Freedom Counseling Services, Media A-Team, Inc.*, March 2002. Web. 7 Dec. 2009. www.hopeandfreedom.com/hidden-pages/private/wounded-clergy.html.

pornography on your own, you will be forced to make certain decisions and compromises in order to keep the battle hidden. These compromises will inevitably lead to shame, isolation, and dishonesty—three strongholds that, when left unchecked, the enemy will use to gain deeper access into your life. This is why it is so important to overcome the false belief that you must fight alone.

Fighting Alone Leads to Shame

We often consider shame and guilt to be the same thing, but it's important to recognize they are actually quite different.

Guilt rises within us as a response to our sin once we realize we have done something wrong. If we have a right view of God and of ourselves, we will understand how He wants to take this guilt from us and grant us His forgiveness. Guilt, ultimately, is meant to show us our need to reach out to Him. If we understand this, we can see how He created guilt as a way to draw us closer to Him.

If Satan has his way, though, he will deceive you into believing these feelings of guilt are the result of God pushing you away because of your sin. He wants you to see your sin through his microscope and believe that because of it, you are worse than everyone else. He wants you to believe that God may be able to forgive others, but certainly not you. This is no longer guilt, though. It's shame, which is yet another way the devil tries to distort something God intends for your good into something that drags you into bondage.

I mentioned earlier how afraid I was of people discovering the truth about my hidden sin. I felt like there was something deeply wrong with *me* because of all the crap in my life I just couldn't get under control. This caused me to feel like even God had turned His back on me. My sin had made me unlovable, unworthy, unacceptable—or so I felt. I saw it as the defining characteristic of who I was, which is what always happens when shame becomes your focal point. But that's not how God saw me. Not at all.

This is the problem with shame. Instead of drawing you closer to God, it causes you to pull away from Him. Rather than placing your focus on God and His forgiveness, it keeps you focused on your sin. It leads you to believe there is something especially wrong with you and, therefore, you must hide from God and others until you can figure out how to become acceptable again.

Fighting Alone Leads to Isolation

This temptation to hide while you try to fix your sin is by no means a new trick. In fact, it's one of the very first lies the devil used to try and separate man from God. After Satan deceived Eve into eating the fruit (and Adam waltzed right into the same trap), we see them reach that moment of clarity that so often comes right after you've given in to a sinful temptation:

> At that moment their eyes were opened, and they suddenly felt shame at their nakedness. So they sewed fig leaves together to cover themselves (Genesis 3:7).

Adam and Eve immediately knew they had done something wrong. But instead of recognizing their guilt and running back to God, they felt shame and tried to cover themselves—to hide—from God and from each other. A short while later, they heard God walking through the garden and suddenly became very aware of the inadequacy of their fig leaves to cover their shame. But again, instead of reaching out for His help, they hid from Him:

> Then the Lord God called to the man, "Where are you?" [Adam] replied, "I heard you walking in the garden, so I hid. I was afraid because I was naked" (Genesis 3:9–10).

Adam and Eve attempted to cover their sinfulness on their own, and when it didn't work, they believed the lie that their sin required them to hide from God until they could figure out how to clean themselves up. But God already knew they had sin in their lives. He knew exactly what they were hiding from Him, and yet He still pursued them. The guilt that Adam and Eve felt immediately after eating the fruit was supposed to draw them back to God, but Satan distorted their perception into shame, which led them to hide from God.

If you believe the lie of shame—that your sin makes you unlovable—and you fear that God and others will reject you if they knew the truth about you, the only option you have is to hide while you clean yourself up. You must remain in isolation until you find a way to become acceptable again. This plays right into the trap of the devil, though, because your sin isn't something you can clean up on your own. In fact, once you go down this road, your sin will only become more central in your day-to-day awareness because of how much time and effort you will be devoting to trying to fix it. Your sinfulness will become your focal point. But the more you focus on your sin, the more gasoline will get dumped onto the fire of your shame. In the same way that shame leads you into isolation, isolation leads to even more shame.

If your journey is anything like mine, you will reach this point and find yourself facing quite a dilemma. I had made a vow in my mind to hide the truth about my sin no matter what, but I also knew I couldn't live my entire life in solitary confinement. I knew I would need to interact with other people at some point, especially those who were closest to me. But sharing my life with others meant an increased risk of being found out. The more I let someone in past the defenses of my isolation, the more likely they were to discover something about me that I wanted to remain hidden.

So what was I to do?

Like most addicts, I became a master of deception and dishonesty.

I became a darn good liar.

Fighting Alone Leads to Dishonesty

People at church would ask me how my life was going, and even though my marriage was falling apart, I was afraid I was about to lose my job and, oh yeah, I was addicted to pornography, I would smile and say, "I'm doing fine." When the guys in my small group were sharing prayer requests, I might share something vague along the lines of "I'm dealing with some… you know…guy stuff. Nothing major. I just figure if you all are praying anyway…it's really not a big deal."

This deception eventually led to rampant dishonesty in all areas of my life. I lied to my wife about everything from how much money I had spent on a new jacket to where I was after work. I lied to cover my tracks online, to justify my laziness at work, and to keep myself in good standing with anyone whose opinion of me I felt mattered. It was exhausting keeping track of all the lies I was telling others. The energy I could have been putting toward loving others was all being directed toward keeping up my never-ending charade.

Whenever my wife asked me why I was so distant, I'd look directly into her tear-filled eyes and tell her I didn't know. But that was a lie, because I knew full well what was going on. When our marriage was falling apart and she asked me why she didn't feel like she could trust me anymore, I told her she *should* trust me and swore I had told her everything. But the truth was, I hadn't told her everything. I had just decided that it was better to keep lying than to allow the truth to surface.

Eventually, I progressed to the point where I no longer felt any guilt about lying as long as it resulted in my own benefit—regardless of how much it was hurting others. Like many who choose to keep certain parts of their life hidden *no matter what*, I had become a pathological liar.

These three results that come from believing you are alone in the battle—shame, isolation, and dishonesty—all feed right into the one decision Satan is hoping you will choose. He wants you to put on a mask in order to appear perfect and vow to hide your imperfections from others at all costs. But this mask you wear to protect yourself will in fact do just the opposite. Instead of providing the buffer you believe is required to make you appear acceptable to others, it will create a barrier that blocks you from ever truly connecting with anyone. It will lead you even further down the road to isolation.

But don't lose heart. Remember that there is a second half to the truth that destroys the lie of this chapter:

TRUTH: You are not the only one fighting this battle, and God never intended for you to fight it alone.

God wants you to reach out for help, but you can't do so unless you allow someone else to become aware that your battle exists in the first place. So, as frightening as it may be, you must take your mask off and allow the truth about your struggle to become known. It's the only way.

Coming Out of Hiding

God's plan for your freedom was never for you to fight in isolation as you remain hidden on your own little island. In fact, He has made it clear that He wants you to reach out for help from others:

> Confess your sins to each other and pray for each other so that you may be healed. The earnest prayer of a righteous person has great power and produces wonderful results (James 5:16).

Did you catch that? If we confess our sins to each other, we will be healed. For some reason, God has decided that He wants the healing of our habitual sins to be a team sport. This makes perfect sense when you think about it. Jesus tells us the defining characteristic of believers that sets us apart from the world is our love.[4] Nothing shows Christlike love to others more than coming alongside a brother who is struggling, sharing your life with him, praying for him, and accepting him regardless of his imperfections. Likewise, it's through these types of relationships that you will begin to experience what the unconditional love of Christ looks like in your own life as well.

One of the major turning points in my struggle with pornography came when I first attended a recovery group at a local church. When I walked through the door that first time, I was scared to death. I remember being afraid I would be rejected because of my sin even though I knew these guys were all struggling with similar stuff. Once I heard them share their stories and came to realize that perhaps my sin wasn't all that different from what they were dealing with, I finally had the courage to come out of hiding and share my own story with them. These guys not only listened to me, but they hugged me, cried with me, and prayed with me. If anything, I felt as if they actually loved me *more* because of my willingness to share openly and honestly with them. Over time, it became easier for me to share my struggles with these men because of their continual love and acceptance. Because I trusted that they would never reject me or condemn me no matter what I struggled with, I actually wanted to come

4 John 13:35.

to them for support. What I realize now is, these men were modeling for me a picture of Christ's unconditional love.

If God *had* answered my prayers to win this battle over pornography while I was still fighting on my own, I would have missed this opportunity to experience His love at work in my life through His church. I would have become self-sufficient and attributed my healing to my own willpower. I definitely wouldn't be here sharing my story, because I guarantee you I would still be hiding that part of my past.

I have now come to understand that God *couldn't* answer that prayer because I was praying against His will. Part of the beauty of the church is how God allows us to be drawn closer to each other through the sharing of our struggles. If He gave us the option of living life on our own and remaining isolated, He would be denying us the opportunity to experience what it means to be part of the body of Christ—one of the most meaningful aspects of life with Him. I believe He loves us too much to let us miss out on something as beautiful as that.

Living in the Light

As terrifying as it was to walk through the doors of a recovery group that first time, I couldn't wait to come back each week after that. That's because once I came out of hiding and my sin was no longer a secret, it began to lose its power within me. I started to experience what it means to live in the light:

> But if we are living in the light, as God is in the light, then we have fellowship with each other, and the blood of Jesus, his Son, cleanses us from all sin (1 John 1:7).

Bringing your sin into the light not only blesses us with true fellowship (like I was experiencing in the recovery group), it also allows your sin to come under the healing power of the cross. Please understand, this is not talking about habitual sins blocking you from eternal salvation. All of your sin—past, present, and future—has been fully paid for by the work of Jesus upon the cross, which means the sin that remains in your life today has already been forgiven. What John is talking about here is the power of *hidden* sin in your life to keep you trapped in darkness today. In other words, the sin you refuse to acknowledge—the sin you are hiding in the dark—will keep you from fully living the life God has designed for you on this Earth. By hiding it you are essentially saying, "I've got this—I can deal with it on my own. I don't need the blood of Jesus to cover it." You may not realize it, but you are choosing to reject the freedom God has promised you in that area.

Living in the Light Breaks the Power of Sin

Once you bring your hidden sin into the light, it loses its power over you. Darkness cannot exist in the presence of light. This is precisely why I encourage men to think beyond the standard definition of an accountability partner. I am fully in favor of having at least one trusted brother you can tell everything to. But what if, instead of waiting to confess a sin until *after* you commit it, you get into the habit of confessing it *before* you commit it? What would happen if you sent a quick text to your trusted brother as you were sitting in front of your computer and still only *thinking* about clicking on a link? Nothing fancy—just something simple like "I'm struggling here. Pray for me. Call me in 10 and make sure I'm okay."

The simple act of bringing the sin into the light (the sin you are only *thinking* about committing at this point), will strip that sin of its power over you before you ever commit it. Did you catch that? You still haven't sinned! This is huge! Just knowing that your struggle isn't hidden, that you have someone praying for you, and that he's going to check in with you will pull you out of the fog of temptation and move you into the spiritual clarity that usually only comes *after* you've sinned. Living in the light is more than just confessing what you have already done; it's confessing even what you are thinking about doing. In this way, the power of a sin can be destroyed by the light before you ever commit it.

I'll give you an example of how this works in my life today. A few weeks back I was doing some software updates on my computer and for some reason, the updates disabled my filter software. I don't know how long it had been down, but eventually I noticed my Internet connection was no longer shutting off at the curfew I've set for myself. I knew I couldn't fix it without having my dad enter the admin password for me, but I wouldn't see him until the following day. Even though I wasn't tempted by anything in that moment, I still realized the temptation could—and likely would—come while the filter was down. (Satan doesn't miss these opportunities to turn up the heat, and we need to be on the lookout for them.) I chose to be proactive and sent a text to a few guys, filling them in on the situation. I asked them to pray for me, check in with me, and make sure I not only resisted the temptation but also got the filter back up and running as soon as possible. Sure enough, the next morning when I woke up, I felt the pull of pornography. I knew full well the filter was down, but because the potential sin had already been brought into the light, it was much easier to resist the temptation.

Living in the Light Sets You Free from Dishonesty

You may not realize it, but if you are still hiding, a significant amount of your energy is being devoted to keeping track of all the lies you have been telling. I didn't realize how exhausting it was to live this way until I experienced the peace that came through stepping into the light. My fear of being exposed was finally over. The peace that came with not having to hide anymore was amazing. Once I started to experience the freedom of honesty, I wanted everything out in the open. I wanted there to be no more secrets in my life.

My biggest fear with stepping into the light was knowing I would need to come clean about all the lies I had been telling to others. I knew the honesty would hurt a lot of people, but I also knew it was what God was calling me to do. I had to reach the point where I realized I had already hurt these people. The honesty wasn't causing them *more* hurt; it was me taking responsibility for the damage I had already caused.

I can tell you now that every confession was absolutely worth it. There were countless times where I was afraid I would be punched in the face for owning up to something I had lied about, but in reality, every one of these conversations ended up being a blessing.

We see something similar happening in the story of Zacchaeus's conversion.[5] When Zacchaeus met Jesus and decided to live in the light, he vowed

---

5 Luke 19.

to pay back everyone he had cheated—four times over! I would have loved to sit in on those interactions and see the looks on people's faces. Imagine if your neighbor knocked on your door one day. With a sheepish look, he tells you the following: "Hey Bro, I stole $20 from you a few years back. Here's $80. I'm sorry I was dishonest and hid the truth from you. I hope you can forgive me." Would you punch him or hug him? Chances are, his confession and honesty might even draw you into a deeper level of friendship. There are no guarantees of how others will respond to you in these situations, but if God is calling you to bring a particular area into the light, He will bless that interaction and use it for the good of His kingdom.

Living in the Light Sets You Free to Influence Others

Whether we like it or not, the world (those who have not trusted in Jesus) is constantly looking at us as representations of what it means to be a follower of Jesus. And it's no surprise that so many people are turned off by what they see.

The world believes that followers of Jesus are really no different than anyone else. They see us as hypocrites, claiming that we are only lying in order to appear as if we are fixed. They look at "Bullhorn Guy" on the college campus telling everyone else they are going to hell while pretending to be perfect himself. They see the pastor who has the hidden affair that becomes a public scandal. They see certain churches pointing out the sins of others in an attempt to take the focus off their own sinfulness. If we attempt to hide our sin to appear perfect, we truly are being hypocrites. So as hard as it is to hear, this accusation is probably justified. Many of us really are hypocrites.

Living in the light, however, opens the door for others to see that following Jesus isn't about being perfect—it's about realizing that we all are broken and need a Savior. We can show others that it's okay to still have issues as a follower of Christ. After all, God doesn't need us to pretend to be perfect in order to make Him look good. In fact, to do so would be to call Him a liar:

> If we claim we have not sinned, we are calling God a liar and showing that his word has no place in our hearts (1 John 1:10).

Our attempts at hiding our sin from others don't make Jesus look more appealing—they actually make following Him look like a sham. For example, many parents will try to appear perfect, hoping their children will see religion as a path to an improved life. But you simply cannot hide your imperfections from someone living under the same roof as you for so many years, no matter how hard you try. The reality is, all kids know that their parents *aren't* perfect. They know Mom and Dad are merely faking it to try and look like they have it all together. Unfortunately, these kids often come to see religion as nothing more than a set of restrictive rules with no real power to change your life. This is a huge reason why so many kids today are walking away from their faith once they leave the home.

But what if parents allowed their kids to see themselves as works in progress just like everyone else? What if parents were honest with their kids about their imperfections, owned up to their struggles, and asked forgiveness from their kids when necessary? I am willing to bet these kids would see Christ at work in their parents' lives and might even be drawn in by their honesty. Perhaps these kids would become comfortable enough in this culture of openness to share their own deep struggles with their parents as well. Isn't that ultimately what every parent hopes for?

Living in the light will benefit every relationship in your life. After all, nothing opens the door to meaningful fellowship more than the willingness to share the real you with others. Openness produces a feeling of safety in other people, enabling them to trust you because they sense that you are choosing to trust them. This relational safety will make it easier for them to step into the light themselves and experience the gift of being known. I can't tell you how many times I have shared my story with a friend only to hear him say, "I've never mentioned this to anyone before, but..." This is why God made His church a team sport.

Fil Anderson sums this all up perfectly:

> My highest hope is for all of us to stop trying to fool others by appearing to have our act together. As people living in intimate union with God, we need to become better known for what and who we actually are. Perhaps a good place to begin would

> be telling the world—before the world does it's own investigating—that we are not as bad as they think. We're worse. At least I know that I'm worse...No matter how boring followers of Jesus may appear to be to the outsiders, they don't know the half of it. Trust me...If we really believe the gospel we proclaim, we'll be honest about our own beauty and brokenness, and the beautiful broken one will make Himself known to our neighbors through the chinks in our armor—and in theirs.[6]

Putting It into Practice

I hope by now you are beginning to see how vitally important it is to come out of hiding and live your life in the light. Perhaps you already know of a trusted brother, or a safe place, where you can begin to do this—a place where you can share your secrets and not be rejected for them. If so, I encourage you to jump in with both feet and thank the Lord for the gift of such a community. But what if you don't know of such a place? The reality is, these places can be hard to find. Sometimes you will find such a place, and sometimes God will call you to create one.

Pornography-Specific Recovery Groups

There are many options for pornography-specific recovery groups, but I am hesitant to give a blanket recommendation for all of them. These groups *may* be a safe community, but they may also feed a performance-based, competition mentality, which will only lead to more hiding. If you sense the group you are attending is putting a large focus on how many days you have been "clean" or how well you are managing your sin, living in the light may actually be subconsciously discouraged. Most men, especially addicts, will be tempted to hide the full depth of their struggle in order to appear to be doing just as fine as the next guy. If there is any sense that you are being graded on an imaginary curve, openness will never thrive.

There are plenty of groups, however, that understand the most important

6 Fil Anderson, *Breaking the Rules*, (Downers Grove, IL: InterVarsity Press, 2010), 81.

gift they can offer to others isn't to fix them, but to simply be a place where nothing needs to remain hidden. They realize true freedom comes as the result of honesty, not performance. These types of groups understand that the main point isn't to plow through curriculum or keep track of performance, but simply to be honest with each other and love guys unconditionally. If you are looking for a group such as this, I would encourage you to check out the Samson Society,[7] or our own small group listing page at beltoftruth.com.[8] Chances are, you will be able to find a group close enough for you to attend.

Some of you may be sensing that God is calling you to start your own recovery group. If so, I would encourage you to talk with your pastor about the possibility of you providing a safe place for other men to come out of hiding. There are some great resources on our Belt of Truth website (including a group guide to accompany this book) that can help you get started as a recovery group leader. Honestly, though, all you really need is a private room and a willingness to love on guys who are struggling.

Infusing a Culture of Honesty into an Existing Group

If you already have a close group of guys you meet with on a regular basis, it may be the best place to start. I've found that a single act of honesty can change the culture of an entire small group from that point forward. Often, these men already sense a desire within themselves to share their struggles openly, but they question whether the group is a safe enough place to do so. If somebody breaks the ice and isn't rejected, the safety is now established and the risk is gone. God may be calling you to be the guy who breaks the ice.

Changing a Culture from the Top

If you are a pastor—or in any position of leadership—you have a unique opportunity to change the culture of your church from the top down. If the benefits of living in the light are taught from the pulpit, they may begin to penetrate the cracks in people's armor and encourage them to come out

---

7 http://samsonsociety.com.

8 http://www.beltoftruth.com/find-group/.

of hiding. If, however, living in the light is *modeled* from the pulpit, it will rock the foundations of the church in an amazing way. Nothing will speak to a congregation more than the pastor coming out of hiding and modeling what a life lived in the light looks like. I'm not saying you need to confess *all* your sins to the entire congregation. You can, however, model vulnerability, openness, and honesty in an appropriate manner if you seek the Lord's wisdom and direction in doing so.

Paul gives us a great example of what honesty from the pulpit might look like:

> This is a trustworthy saying, and everyone should accept it: "Christ Jesus came into the world to save sinners"—and I am the worst of them all. *But God had mercy on me so that Christ Jesus could use me as a prime example of his great patience with even the worst sinners.* Then others will realize that they, too, can believe in him and receive eternal life (1 Timothy 1:15–16).

I understand this idea may be hard for pastors to get excited about. The reality is, the more influence you have, the more tempting it will be to hide who you really are. This is why it's hard for me to admit my own struggles to the guys I'm working with. I want to influence them, but I am afraid they won't listen to me if I admit I'm not perfect. The level of honesty within a group, however, is established more by the leader than any other individual. If the leadership of a church doesn't actively pursue a culture of openness and honesty, hiddenness will be the natural bent of the congregation. Most interactions on a Sunday morning will be people sharing how "fine" they are while they pretend to be perfect. Your church will feel more like a country club than a family. This is why it's so important for you to set the example for others.

Regardless of what you decide to share from the pulpit, I would strongly suggest you still seek out a core group of men who really can know *everything* about you. There are many men in ministry who remain shackled to hidden sin because so few of them have found a safe place to share their struggles without the risk of losing their jobs. But it's important that you find help somewhere, even if it means joining a recovery group at another church, because remaining in isolation will cripple your relationship with Christ as well as your effectiveness in ministry.

If I could go back and do my life over again, I would never choose to hide my sin in the first place. I can see now that the hiding was never worth it—not even in the least. For this reason, I am confident that once you experience the freedom that comes from living in the light, you too will wonder why you ever chose to hide your sin in the first place. This doesn't make it any easier to do what you may feel the Lord calling you to do, though, which is why I encourage you to ask Him for the strength to follow His leading and begin to live in the light.

Jesus, please give me the strength to bring my sins into the light and let the truth about me be known. Please provide a trusted friend, or a safe community, where others can love me with your unconditional love—no matter what I bring to the table. I want to trust your Word when it says that confessing to one another will lead me to freedom. Please give me the faith required to live such a life where nothing needs to remain hidden. I trust your blood to cover me. Thank you, Lord.

LIE #3

My Pornography Addiction is About Fulfilling My Sexual Desires

Sex education may be a good idea in the schools, but I don't believe the kids should be given homework.

BILL COSBY

I graduated high school in 1997 at the wise age of 17. My sole criteria for selecting a college was that it not be in my hometown, mainly so I would have an excuse to move out of my parents' house and live on my own. I was accepted to Oregon State University and soon found myself living out in the real world before I was even old enough to buy cigarettes.

My life really began to separate into two personas during my college years. On the surface, I was "Steve the church guy," going to Bible studies and maintaining a facade of moralistic perfection. Under the surface, though, I was a completely different person. I had an entirely different group of friends who I would party with on weekends, often driving up I-5 to all-night raves in Portland where we would fry our brains with a cocktail of illegal drugs. I embraced the freedom of no longer having a curfew (or any house rules), and reacted like a dog being released from his cage. The lack of boundaries in my life fueled more than just my party lifestyle. It fueled the flames of my pornography addiction as well, causing it to grow into a raging inferno.

LIE #3: My Pornography Addiction is About Fulfilling My Sexual Desires

The Internet was still a novelty in the '90s. Prior to college, I had only experienced it at friends' houses. But now I had 24/7 access and a room with a lock on the door. This was not a good combination. Actually, that is an understatement. It was more like pouring gasoline on the fire of my addiction. I would lock my door each night once my roommate went to bed, plant myself in front of the computer, and surf porn sites until I couldn't stay awake any longer. What used to take 10 minutes to download now took 10 seconds. Instead of seeing two or three images a night, I was suddenly able to view thousands. I felt as if I had won the pornography lottery. But no matter how long I looked, I could never get enough. I was always searching for the elusive "perfect image" that would fully satisfy me.

I always knew in my heart that this lifestyle was wrong. I begged God to take my sex drive away until marriage. I made promises to Him. I installed an Internet filter. I tried everything to stop, but nothing worked.

It wasn't long before I lost any hope of finding freedom from pornography. I began to believe that I had a sex drive that was significantly more intense than other guys and there wasn't anything I could do to control it. God had apparently created me to require a release multiple times a day, and at least porn was a better option than sleeping around. My best chance at freedom, in my mind, was to get married. I believed that once I was married I would be permitted to have sex with my wife whenever I wanted and would therefore no longer need pornography. These thoughts were all lies.

As men, we tend to believe our struggles with pornography are purely about sexual desire. If this were the case, though, my addiction *would* have gone away once I was married. So why is it my addiction actually became worse within marriage? Why did I repeatedly choose to reject the advances of my beautiful, attractive, and loving wife in order to get my sexual needs met through pornography? The only answer that makes sense is that pornography addiction isn't actually the result of an overzealous libido. It's also not about an underattentive spouse, a lack of willpower, or even sexual desire. Pornography addiction is the result of being too afraid to risk anything in the process of trying to meet the deepest needs of your soul. The problem with porn, though, is it can never make good on its promise. In fact, it will pull you away from the very things that truly can meet those deepest needs.

TRUTH: Pornography addiction is an attempt to meet the deepest needs of your soul without being required to risk anything in the process.

What are Your Deepest Needs?

God has placed within the heart of every man the need to be validated as a man, the need for adventure in his life, and the need to experience intimacy with others. These needs are not sinful in and of themselves, but we often attempt to satisfy them in sinful ways—such as through pornography.

In order to meet these needs effectively, you will be required to take risks. And risk, by its very nature, carries the potential for failure. Because of this reality, Satan will try to deceive you into finding an easier way to meet these needs. He wants you to believe that you can be fulfilled in these areas without having to put yourself on the line. Lasting and effective solutions will only be found in the truth, though, which is why it is so important to understand each of these needs within you and recognize how pornography will never be able to truly fulfill any of them.

The Need to Be Validated as a Man

I've noticed a growing interest in "manly" things in the past few years. First, it was just "Mustache March." But now we have "No Shave November" and "Beardtober" as well. Here in the northwest, hipsters dress like urban lumberjacks and listen to bands with names like Grizzly Bear and Blitzen Trapper. We are told Chuck Norris can cut through a hot knife with butter, swim through land, and cure cancer with his tears (if he ever cried).[1] As if that isn't ridiculous enough, you can now buy beer bottled inside of a taxidermy squirrel.[2] Manliness is apparently making quite a comeback.

I must confess, I love manly stuff as much as the next guy. I have a beard, I've been known to wear flannel, and I consider red meat to be the base of the food pyramid. But I have also learned that manly things do not make you a man. If that were the case, any woman who loves bacon,

1 www.chucknorrisfacts.com.

2 http://eater.com/archives/2010/07/22/beer-in-a-squirrel-brewdog-unveils-strongest-most-expensive-beer-ever.php.

beer, and a good action movie would also qualify as a man. (I'd say if anything, she qualifies as a keeper.) So what is it that truly makes you a man?[3]

The thing that makes you a man is your masculinity—specifically, *biblical* masculinity. As John Piper explains in his book *Recovering Biblical Masculinity*, you must understand that being a man is accepting God's call to live your life walking in "Benevolent Responsibility."

A Biblical Man Offers Benevolence...

Benevolence is the sacrificial giving of yourself, your strength, and your abilities to others. We see this theme repeated all throughout the Scriptures. God calls husbands to love their wives in the same way Christ loves the church, to the point of laying down their lives for them.[4] Isaiah rebukes the leaders of Sodom and Gomorrah for not helping the oppressed, defending orphans, or fighting for the rights of widows.[5] In other words, not using their masculine strength to help those who are weak.

How often do we see Jesus, our example of true masculinity, modeling benevolence in His interactions with the outcasts of society? Jesus didn't need to touch the leper physically in order to heal Him (He healed others with words alone), but He chose to give up His rights to cleanliness and sanitation in order to give the man something he needed more than physical healing. He offered this man love and acceptance.[6]

Or what about the woman at the well? The town surely knew her reputation as an immoral woman, yet Jesus still spoke with her one on one, fully aware of the inevitable gossip. On top of that, it was against the cultural norm for a Jew to interact with a Samaritan, yet Jesus ignored that custom as well. He was willing to risk rumors and judgment against Him in order to give this woman what she desperately needed—hope, salvation, and Him.[7] This is true benevolence.

---

3 I know where your mind is going. The answer is no. Your external plumbing does not make you a *man*—it merely makes you a *male*.

4 Ephesians 5:25–27.

5 Isaiah 1:17.

6 Luke 5:12–16.

7 John 4:1–26.

A Biblical Man Accepts Responsibility...

God will never burden you with a responsibility that is too great for you. He will, however, give you responsibilities that will challenge you to grow as a man. This is one of the main purposes of responsibility, and it's why we see God entrusting men with responsibilities from the very beginning:

> The LORD God took the man and put him in the Garden of Eden to work it and keep it (Genesis 2:15).

The Hebrew words used here for "work" and "keep" are translated elsewhere in the Bible as "serve" and "guard." God placed the entire garden under Adam's authority, trusting him with the responsibility to serve it and guard it. If God had never given Adam a job to do and left him to play fetch with the dingoes all day, he would never have had a reason to grow or mature. In the same way, God will place things under your authority and ask you to serve and guard them as well. Not because He wants to fill your time with meaningless tasks, but because He wants you to be challenged in ways that will lead to true masculinity.

One obvious example of this, for many men, is their family. Men are called to serve their families by providing for them,[8] and to guard their families by leading them spiritually and setting appropriate boundaries for their protection. This same responsibility to serve and to guard may pertain to your job, your ministry, or anything else God has entrusted you with as well.

But Men Are Afraid They Won't Be Able to Answer the Call

Many men have an underlying fear that they won't be able measure up to what is being asked of them. Whether it is a call for their strength and goodness (benevolence), or their service and protection (responsibility), many men fear they won't have what it takes. You might fail. You may let people down. You could offend someone. Unfortunately, when men fear failure, they tend to avoid even showing up in the first place. They hide from conflict, run away from risk, and watch their true masculinity die a slow death within them.

---

8 1 Timothy 5:8.

If this becomes the pattern of your life, you will always feel a need to "prove yourself" as a man. The death of your masculinity will leave a void within you. Sometimes men will try to fill this void and prove their masculinity through sports or other manly hobbies. Frequently, it's by climbing higher up the corporate ladder. Unfortunately, it's often sought through the pursuit of a woman, which commonly manifests as an affair. Either way, you will forever be seeking external validation, because the true validation of your masculinity that you desire will remain unmet.

It's here, in this moment, where pornography becomes the attractive answer—or at least it seems like the answer.

The less a man feels like a real man, the more vulnerable he is to the lure of pornography. One of the foundational lies behind porn is that you will never be asked to prove your worth or give anything of yourself to be seen as a man. The world of porn is full of beautiful women who seem to be saying, "Hey Stud…I desire you just as you are. You're masculine enough for me." In this way, porn offers you the same validation as an affair, but without the same risk. Which is why men turn to pornography to experience the rush of endorphins, the sense of untamed strength that comes with an erection, and the validation of being desired by a woman—all without taking the necessary risks of true, biblical masculinity.

It's yet another way Satan replaces God's solution with a cheap counterfeit that will never satisfy.

The worst part of this, is pornography doesn't just deceives you, it actually pulls you further away from the only thing that will satisfy your need for masculine validation in your life, which is to live as the man God has called you to be. Or to put it another way, pornography keeps you from living in biblical masculinity.

Porn never asks you to give of yourself out of benevolence. In fact, it does exactly the opposite. Porn makes you selfish because the sole focus is on *your* needs, *your* wants, and *your* pleasure—even at the risk of causing pain to others. Furthermore, instead of offering your strength to protect others, you are participating in the exploitation of women. If you are married, you aren't selflessly protecting your wife; you are selfishly hurting her heart. I am not trying to guilt you here. I am just pointing out the ugly truth behind Satan's apparent "solution" to this need for validation within you.

It doesn't matter how many belching contests you win, how thick your facial hair grows in, or how many flesh-colored pixels on a computer monitor appear to desire you—you will still need to come back to these things repeatedly to attempt to receive validation as a man. If, however, you are willing to risk yourself for the good of others and accept responsibility for what God has placed under your authority, then you will begin to experience lasting validation as the man He created you to be.

The best part is, God has *already* made you the man He wants you to be. You don't need to make yourself into someone new or become stronger than you already are. You can trust that you are man enough simply because God says you are man enough.

The Need for Adventure in Your Life

If you ask a man what his favorite movies are, you will more than likely get a list of classics such as *Lord of the Rings, Indiana Jones, Iron Man,* and other movies involving swords and explosions. Few men will add *Sleepless in Seattle* or *The Notebook* to their Netflix queue unless an attractive female wants to watch it with them. When was the last time you heard a guy say, "Hey bro, wanna grab a pizza and watch *Notting Hill*?" Probably never. So why is it the majority of men all seem to like the same types of movies?

Perhaps it's because these movies awaken the deep sense of adventure that God has placed in your masculine soul.

Adventures are exciting because you are forced to figure out the answers as you go along. The outcome—and often the path—is unknown. You don't know how it's going to end. There may be danger involved. Failure is a possibility. Driving to the grocery store to pick up a gallon of milk is not an adventure. Finding the grocery store on fire and running in to rescue people is. Which scenario gets you more excited as a man? I can't be the only one who fantasizes about things such as rescuing people from burning buildings or fighting off mountain lions on the trail. It's written in our hearts as men.

When I was a boy, I was constantly searching for mud and dirt and doing all the typical things little boys do. I would drive my go-kart up and down the road wearing a swim mask while pretending to be an astronaut. I joined the Boy Scouts and daydreamed about building the hovercraft advertised on the back page of *every* issue of *Boys Life* magazine. As I got older, I did all the stuff teenage boys with a lack of any common sense consider to be adventure. I bombed down hills on my bike so fast I'd pass the driving cars. I found out that my 1976 AMC Pacer speedometer pegged at 90, but the car still accelerated for quite a while after that. Even today, as an adult, there is little that makes me feel more alive than hiking, climbing, or skiing in the mountains of Oregon.

I have always been aware of this desire for adventure inside me, but I misunderstood the root of it for many years. You see, adventure isn't just about getting an adrenaline fix or doing something worthy of a YouTube video. It's about being *alive*. God created men to desire adventure because the skills we learn through it—endurance, perseverance, trust, risk—are the same skills we need to experience a life fully alive to Him. After all, the greatest adventure of all—the *only* adventure that will fully meet this need within a man—is the adventure of living by faith.

But what happens if you ignore or reject your desire for adventure, refuse to take risks, and choose to live a "safe" life? Life will become nothing more than punching a clock, doing your daily duties, and only saying the "right" things so you don't stir the pot. Men who accept this life become passive... jaded...bored. When these men see a burning building, they drive right past it and look for the safer grocery store. They've become perfectly content with just picking up the milk—even if they have to go elsewhere.

It's here, once again, where Satan sweeps in with his own "solution." Instead of adventure, though, he offers something much safer—something free from risk. He offers fantasy.

Accepting Fantasy as a Substitute for Adventure

Fantasy is the opposite of adventure. Instead of awakening life within you, it encourages you to hide from life. It promises an escape from the pain and disappointment in your *real* world that you are too afraid to face. Instead of embracing the risk of addressing these things and entering into the adventure of faith that God has called you to, you check out. You turn to the TV, to video games, or often to the computer as a means of distracting yourself from the hard realities of real life. But these distractions are not real. They are merely fantasies.

The power of pornography thrives within this fantasy world. After all, every man feels like Brad Pitt on the Internet. The women are willing and eager to do whatever you want, whenever you want. They won't ask you how your day went at work or how things are going at home. They will never bring up the painful stuff. They won't ask you about your insecurities or fears. There is no risk of them rejecting you. You can find a retreat from the imperfect reality of your life, sweep your pain under the rug, and run away with the girl of your dreams to live happily ever after. Or so the lie goes.

There is no way around the fact that life will be hard at times. Bosses can yell at you. Your wife may pull away from you. People you don't even know might attack you for your faith. After all, Jesus warned us the world would hate us. He was raising people from the dead and healing the sick, and the world still murdered Him. Why would we assume it will go any better for us? The reality is, we live in a fallen, broken, hurting world full of pain and suffering.

But as men, God has called us to stand firm in our faith and trust in Him, no matter how hard life gets. He wants you to fight for what is good and right, even in your own life. So please, my brother, stop running away from the adventure and hiding in your "safe" fantasy world. There is no life there. Be honest with yourself and ask what makes your heart come alive more: Fighting for your family at all cost, or sitting in front of a computer with your pants around your ankles? It's like asking if you'd rather watch *Return of the King* or *Sex in the City,* isn't it?

The real world needs your strength. Your family needs your strength. And the only way to start believing you have it is to trust God when He calls you to run toward the burning building. Yes, you may get singed in places, but it's worth it.

The Need to Experience Intimacy with Others

When we hear the word "intimacy," we often think of it confined within the box of sexuality. Yes, sexual intimacy is one of the greatest pictures of intimacy between two people, but it's not the full definition. Intimacy is defined more completely as the result of being *fully* known and *fully* knowing another. It's the driving force behind every friendship, relationship, marriage, and community. It's also the very core of what we were created for:

> Jesus replied, "'You must love the Lord your God with *all* your heart, *all* your soul, and *all* your mind.' This is the first and greatest commandment. A second is equally important: 'Love your neighbor as yourself.' The entire law and all the demands of the prophets are based on these two commandments" (Matthew 22:37–40).

We were created to love God and love others *fully*. Or, to put it another way, our souls deeply desire intimacy with God as well as intimacy with others. However, if this need for intimacy isn't being met in your life, nothing else will matter to you. To paraphrase what Jesus said in the previous verse, everything hinges on this.

This may sound like lovey-dovey hippie stuff—*it's all about the love man... puff, puff*—but this is huge. If you are anything like most men, your need for intimacy is *the* driving force behind your struggle with pornography. Once you begin to understand the truth behind this need—and how you are using pornography to try to meet it—you will begin to experience what true intimacy feels like, possibly for the first time in your life. And once you experience true intimacy, you will begin to see how empty and damaging the lie of pornography really is.

I deeply desired to be loved during the years of my addiction, but I had believed the lie that I was unlovable. I came to the conclusion that my only option to ever receive love was to lie and pretend to be someone I wasn't. So, as we saw in the previous chapter, I created a mask—a false self—that I could hide behind and pretend to be worthy of love.

There was one serious flaw with this logic, though. By only allowing people to see my mask, the real me could never receive their love. In fact, the people I desperately wanted to be loved by couldn't love me, not because of their lack of ability or willingness, but because my mask was deflecting their attempts. I knew deep down that any love from others was being directed toward the fake me and not the real me. By keeping my mask on and not allowing anyone to see my struggles, I never gave anyone the chance to love me in spite of those struggles.

I had convinced myself I had to hide the truth about me from my wife in order to at least appear worthy of her love. This constant hiding and dishonesty caused me to feel as if I needed to walk on eggshells around her at all times. I blamed these feelings on her, though, and believed the reason I didn't feel love or acceptance from her was because she wasn't giving me what I needed. I blamed our lack of relational intimacy on her inability to love me correctly, not my inability to receive her love. Of course, I couldn't see this at the time, so I kept trying to find ways to change her behavior toward me instead of looking at what I needed to change on my end.

This same pattern played out with my relationship with God as well. I hid my sin from God and somehow convinced myself it was making me more acceptable. I put on my "Perfect Steve Mask" and volunteered in church, trying to distract God from my sin through service and self-sacrifice. I completely missed the reality that He simply wanted me to be honest about who I was so He could love the *real* me.

So there I was, desperate for love and acceptance—desperate to experience true intimacy—but unable to receive what was being offered to me because of the mask I was wearing. Like many men, though, I believed the lie that my loneliness was the result of no one in my life offering love and acceptance to me, so I began to seek to fulfill these needs elsewhere.

Seeking to Meet Your Need for Intimacy through Pornography

The lure of porn is more about being desired than satisfying your own sexual desires. The rush you get from porn is the same rush you get during that first kiss. We can call it butterflies, infatuation, whatever—but it all comes down to the wonderful experience of knowing you are desired. If you don't believe me, ask yourself what thoughts went through your head after a first kiss. Chances are, it was something more along the lines of *I can't believe she kissed me!* rather than *I can't believe I finally got to kiss her!* Maybe I'm different here, but I doubt it.

Porn gives you that same feeling of being desired, but instead of sensing that the desire is for your mask, you believe the desire is truly meant for you. These women on the screen are fully aware of your pornography addiction (after all, you're looking at them, right?), and yet they still want to be with you. So, in a twisted way, it almost feels like they are the only ones who are loving the real you. The most sinister part of this is that you will begin to crave the affection of pornography more than the affection of real people because this deception appears to be meeting your need for intimacy better than any other relationship.

This is the lie Satan wants you to believe—that pornography will never judge you, condemn you, or push you to be a better person. It will never ask you to shave or shower before being accepted romantically. You can come in from a weeklong backpacking trip, covered in dirt and smelling like a moose, and the women of porn will still desire you just as you are. It doesn't even matter what you are hiding—porn still wants you. It offers you all the benefits of a romantic relationship without the risk of being discovered as a fraud. Better yet, the women of porn couldn't care less if you are a fraud. It doesn't even matter to them. This apparent unconditional acceptance makes it incredibly tempting for men—especially broken, hidden, shame-filled men—to run to the arms of pornography rather than the arms of their spouse or their Creator.

But when you seek intimacy through pornography, it actually produces a very opposite effect in your life. More than likely, every time you turn to porn, you will experience shame, which will feed your feelings of insecurity, not measuring up, and wanting to hide the truth about you. This causes you to add one more memory to your list of reasons you believe no one will love you, which encourages you to tighten the strap on your mask a few more notches. The counterfeit intimacy of pornography becomes an industrial epoxy, gluing your mask—the very thing keeping you from experiencing true intimacy—to your soul even tighter. This is how pornography addiction becomes a cycle that feeds itself.

So how do you stop the downward spiral of pornography addiction and the damage it causes in your life? The answer is simple, but it's not easy. It may very well be the hardest thing you have ever done. The only thing

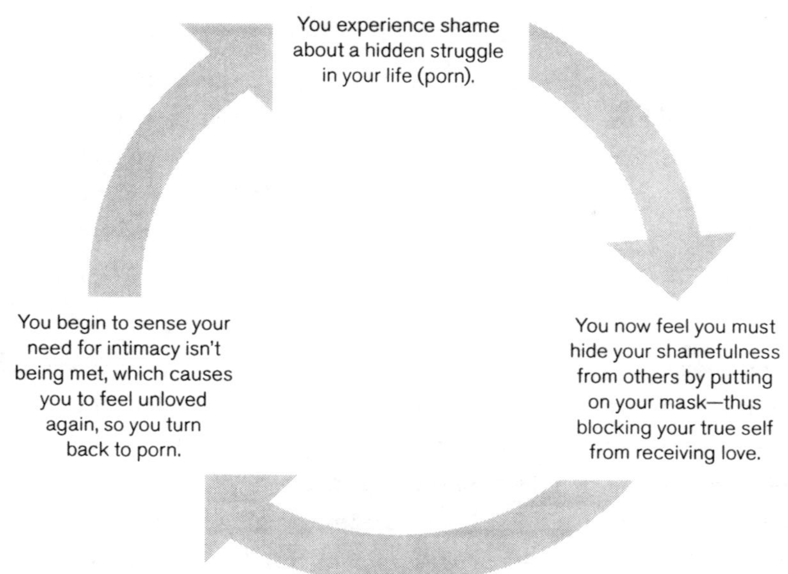

that can stop this cycle is to overcome the shame that is driving it. And the only way to overcome shame is to allow yourself to be fully known, and then realize you are fully loved and accepted in spite of your imperfections.

But to experience this, you must take off your mask and let the real you be known. There is no other way. Don't lose heart, though. This will be one of the most significant and meaningful journeys of your life.

The Path to True Intimacy

I shared in the previous chapter how I never experienced unconditional love or acceptance until I was honest about my struggles with a group of trusted men. It was the first time I felt loved for who I truly was. These men actually loved the *real* me. I slowly began to believe that God loved and accepted the real me in the same way as well. I started to recognize that I didn't need to hide my sin from God. This understanding allowed me to finally believe that it might be possible to live my life without wearing a mask—to let the real me be known.

I love the way Nate Larkin explains how he came to see this reality in his own life:

> I always felt bad that I wasn't a better person. I even created this false self, this "Saint Nate" that I tried to make breathe on its own. I felt bad that "Saint Nate" could only live at church. Now I know that Jesus never loved "Saint Nate" because He didn't make "Saint Nate." He made me. Jesus loves me! He wants a relationship with me! And that's the only real relationship there is.[9]

Did you catch that? Jesus loves *you*! Not your mask. He loves the real you! If you haven't been experiencing His love in your life, it's not because He isn't offering it to you. It's probably because you've been pulling an Adam and trying to hide from Him in the bushes. You've let your mask become a wall that blocks the real you from receiving the love of Christ. Your mask can't receive His love because your mask isn't real. Jesus is waiting for you to be honest with Him about your true self. Cry out to Him. Tell Him who you really are. He already knows the truth anyway. Unload your heart before God—sin and all. Claim it. Confess it. Own it. You will find that He's been there all along, waiting for you to let Him love you in spite of all of it.

The most incredible feeling of acceptance is realizing that the Creator of the universe loves you, even at your worst. God knew you would be right where you are in this moment—pornography and all—and He still chose to send His Son to die for you. Jesus knew you would be here as well, and He still went through with it. When you begin to understand this, any feeling you have of being unlovable or unacceptable will begin to melt away. Once you experience His love and acceptance, your heart will come alive. Your deep need for intimacy will finally be satisfied.

A Word to the Married Men

Even if you aren't married yet, please read this because it may save you from massive heartache in the future. Fair warning, though: You are fully

9 www.youtube.com/watch?v=N3KSWYYJqyo.

accountable for what you know. You won't be able to unlearn what you're about to read. It may haunt you until you deal with it, but it's all part of God's plan to make you the man—and the husband—that He wants you to be.

Still here? Good.

If you are hiding your pornography addiction from your wife, it is more than likely causing her to feel distant from you. She probably senses that there is something wrong with your relationship but has no idea what it is. There will likely come a point where she will ask you why the two of you aren't close (if she hasn't already). In order to keep the truth hidden, you will need to lie.

If you claim to have no answer, she will assume the issue must be with her. This was the path I chose in my marriage, and it's one of the greatest regrets of my life. I watched my wife's happiness deteriorate before me as she frantically tried to figure out whatever it was she was doing wrong in our marriage. Continuing to lie and withholding my true self from her was perhaps the most selfish thing I've ever done. How could I approach my wife, who was hurting so deeply, and ask her to love me when I knew my sin was the true reason she was hurting? I couldn't. So I tightened my mask and went back to porn.

But here's the deal. You will *never* experience intimacy with your spouse if *anything* remains hidden. Anything. True intimacy requires being fully known, and you cannot be fully known if you are withholding any information about who you are. Any lie or hiding, no matter how insignificant it may seem, will destroy the intimacy in your marriage. By attempting to protect yourself and appear worthy of acceptance, you are actually creating an environment where intimacy *cannot* exist. The world will tell you there are secrets you take to the grave, but we are not of the world. You must confess your lies and hiding to your spouse or your marriage will never thrive.

I would encourage you to prayerfully ask God to reveal to you anything you are hiding that is standing in the way of your intimacy as a couple. There may be some extremely difficult things you will need to confess to your wife, but please trust God as He brings these things to your mind. I'd encourage you to talk over your list with your pastor or a counselor first. They can help you develop a plan, offer suggestions on how to proceed, and provide accountability so you are less likely to back out. Above all else, pray about how God wants you to handle this in order to minimize the damage as much as possible.

There will never be a "good" time to confess these things to your spouse. No matter when you do it, it will be hard. But the longer you put it off, the worse the damage will be. I would suggest mentioning to your wife that you have some difficult things you need to discuss and asking her when she would be ready to sit down and discuss them. Be prepared to do it right then if that is her preference. This will hopefully eliminate at least some of her feelings of being blindsided.

There are no guarantees of how this will go—other than it being extremely hard and painful. Make no mistake—this will be a bomb going off in your marriage. You will need the help and support of others to survive this. But the reality is, if your marriage has been built on deception, the foundation is nothing more than a Jenga tower. You can live the rest of your life taking a block from the bottom and moving it to the top, but the wall will only be getting weaker. The only way to truly fix the foundation of your marriage is to rebuild it on a firm foundation of openness and honesty. However, understand that this confession isn't about magically fixing your marriage overnight. It will be like ripping a scab off an infected wound to let it drain and heal properly. It's a disgusting image, but it's unfortunately accurate.

Once the wound has been cleansed and you both begin the long and tender process of healing in a new environment of transparency, you will hopefully begin to experience the seeds of intimacy in your marriage for the first time. You will realize that any love you are receiving from your spouse is being offered to the real you. She now knows everything about you—warts and all—and is still choosing to love you. The energy you previously spent keeping your mask on is now freed up to protect, serve, and lead her—all of which will encourage you in your true masculinity. You will constantly be thankful and grateful for her forgiveness, which will pour out of you as love. To paraphrase Jesus, the more you've been forgiven, the more you love.[10] These are just a few of the many reasons why

10 Luke 7:47.

marriages that survive trials such as these have the potential to become the strongest marriages.

We cannot ignore the very real possibility that your marriage may not heal from this. But the truth is, the pain that your confession will bring up is already present in your marriage—it just hasn't been labeled yet. The damage was done when the sin was committed. Confession is what will allow you to finally accept responsibility for that pain. It will allow your wife to understand what she—and your marriage—will need to heal from. It will allow her to stop blaming herself. If, however, you choose to continue hiding things from her, you will only be causing her more pain. You will be choosing your own desire for control and safety over her happiness and emotional stability. Your marriage may remain intact, but it will never be healthy.

I wish I could say I took my mask off, confessed everything to my wife, and we lived happily ever after. However, as you know from "My Story" at the beginning of this book, it took me a long time to gain the courage to be completely honest with her about all of my lies and selfishness. Ironically, my continual lying and deception—the very things I was doing to protect myself—were ultimately major factors in what pushed her away. In the end, I don't believe she left because of my pornography addiction or even because of my adultery. I believe she left because she couldn't trust me. I had lied to her about who I was for far too long.

By waiting until after we were already separated to come clean about everything, I never gave her the chance to see God working in me. By the time I finally faced the full reality of the pain I'd caused her, it was too late. In her mind, our whole marriage had been a lie. The man she thought she'd married didn't even exist. The only "truth" she knew about me was that I had been willing to sacrifice her well-being for my own protection.

I truly believe that if I had told her everything when I first felt God leading me to come clean, things would have been different. We still would have been living together in the same house at the time, and I believe she would have been more likely to witness the changes that God was working in my heart. She might not have been able to trust me, but perhaps she would have been able to trust the signs of God working within me.

But even if I knew back then what the end results of my confession would be, I still would have gone through with it. In fact, I would have done it much sooner, because confessing everything to her ended up being the single biggest turning point of my life. It was the moment that I finally trusted God and began to experience the true intimacy I had been looking for.

Don't get me wrong here. I hate how much pain my addiction caused my wife over the years. I pray daily that God would heal the pain that I have caused in her heart and remain hopeful that someday, she may even be healed to the point where she becomes open to reconciliation. But even if she doesn't, I know that God will provide me—and her—with all the love and intimacy our souls will ever need.

Why Doesn't Pornography Addiction Go Away Once You're Married?

When you are living with an addiction in the close relationship of a marriage, it becomes significantly more difficult to hide the truth about you. You will find yourself having to work extremely hard to keep your mask of perfection on. It will require more deception, more lies, and more selfishness—all of which will drive a deep wedge between you and your spouse. The intimacy you were hoping to experience in marriage will not be there, and deep down you will know the reason why. You will eventually come to recognize your addiction is no longer hurting just you—it's hurting the woman you love as well.

This all leads to more and more shame, which in turn drives you back to more pornography. Before you even see it coming, you will find yourself attempting to meet your need for intimacy through pornography because the thought of pursuing your wife and being rejected (or worse, exposed) is too much for you to bear.

Which is why pornography addiction doesn't just go away when you are married. If anything, it will get worse.

How Does This Help Me with Porn?

The more you understand the truth about what's really fueling your desire for pornography, and the more you recognize how God wants to satisfy those desires for you fully, the less likely you will be to seek fulfillment through cheap and damaging substitutes.

If you find yourself seeking to be desired by a woman as a means to validate your masculinity, stop and consider if that's truly what you need. Perhaps what you are experiencing isn't the starvation of your masculinity, but the misalignment of it. Once you realign your masculinity with what God has called you to, you will find those false desires beginning to disappear.

The more you embrace the adventures God places in front of you, the more likely you will be to recognize how He uses them to strengthen you as a man. Your desire to turn toward pornography and fantasy for "safe" adventures will diminish because you will be experiencing the true and fulfilling adventures that come with a life of faith.

The next time you are drawn toward pornography because you feel alone, stop and ask yourself where your loneliness is really coming from. Is it the result of nobody in your life offering you love, or is it the result of you hiding behind a mask and not allowing your true self to receive love? If you can trust God enough to remove your mask and allow Him to love the real you, you will begin to experience true intimacy in your soul, which will free you from the need to seek it from pornography.

I encourage you to ask the Lord to reveal to you the truth behind what is driving your addiction. Chances are, it's related to one of these three areas: your masculinity, your desire for adventure, or loneliness. Once you discover the real needs you are trying to meet through pornography, ask God how He wants to meet them for you in appropriate ways. Whatever His answer is, it will likely require you to trust Him in ways you have never trusted Him before. It will be worth it, though. No matter what He calls you to, it will be an adventure. But remember, you were made for adventure.

Father, please give me opportunities to offer my strength to others and the desire to take care of the things you have entrusted to me. Help me to satisfy my thirst for adventure through following you rather than through the things of this world. Please grant me the courage to take off my mask and to allow the real me to be known so I can experience the blessings of true intimacy. Above all else, Lord, please remind me daily how much you love and accept me, even in spite of my imperfections, so I won't be tempted to seek that love and acceptance elsewhere. Thank you, Father.

LIE #4

I Can Compensate for My Pornography Addiction by Doing Enough Good in Other Areas

I'm good enough, I'm smart enough, and doggonit, people like me!

STUART SMALLEY

I've got good news and bad news. The good news: God is good. The bad news, however: You are bad.

Now wait a minute, you may be saying. *I'm a good person!* I'm sure you are in comparison to a lot of other folks. But it doesn't matter where *you* place yourself along the curve of good or bad. The only thing that matters is how God sees you. And God makes it pretty clear in the Bible that He doesn't judge us based on good or bad—He judges us based on perfect or imperfect.[1] You may be able to justify and convince yourself that you're a good person, but no one can honestly call themselves perfect. So the question isn't "Am I a good person?" The question is "Am I good enough?" And because God's requirement is perfection, none of us will ever be good enough to earn our own way into heaven.

TRUTH: None of us will ever be good enough to earn our own way into Heaven.

1 Matthew 5:48.

What does getting into heaven have to do with your pornography struggles? It has *everything* to do with it. In order to ever get free from pornography, you need to start looking at it in the same way God looks at it. He sees your pornography habit as just one part of a much bigger issue in your life—the issue of your sinful nature and the eternal separation from Him that comes with it. So in one sense, porn isn't even the real issue. Sin is the real issue. Until we figure out how to deal with the overall problem of sin in your life in a way that pleases God, focusing on the pornography will be a useless battle. After all, what good would it be if you found a way to overcome pornography in this world only to die and find you are still separated from God for all eternity?

This chapter isn't going to be much fun, but it's a necessary step. The next chapter will hopefully open your eyes to the very good news, which more than makes up for this bad news. I would encourage you to read this chapter and the following chapter together. The next chapter will only make sense after you understand what you're about to see here.

Perhaps an illustration would help explain all of this. Imagine you receive an envelope in the mail one day. As you read the letter inside you find out you've been found guilty of committing a crime—however, some kind benefactor has decided to not only pay your fine, but has also agreed to serve your mandatory prison sentence for you as well. This is all a bit odd, because you weren't even aware you had committed a crime. You don't even know what the crime was—or the penalty for that matter—because the letter never mentioned it. At least you don't have to worry about it, though, because it's all been paid for. And so you go on with your day and don't think much about it.

Now, imagine the same scenario. Only this time the letter contains a lot more detail. As you read it, you realize you have been found guilty of tax evasion. Not only that, it has been going on for years. Because of back taxes and fines, you now owe the IRS over $500,000! Your entire net worth is pennies compared to the fine. You can barely make a dent in it, and can never, ever pay the complete fine. In addition, the minimum prison sentence is ten years.

You show up at the trial and realize there is substantial evidence against you. Financial records, invoices, previous tax returns—it's all there. You have no case. You plead with the judge, claiming it was an accident and you honestly had no idea you were doing anything wrong. He sternly reminds you that ignorance is no excuse for criminal behavior. You broke the law and now you must pay the consequence. The gavel slams against the desk as he sentences you to the maximum prison term in addition to your fine.

As you are being escorted out of the courtroom, however, a man stands up and approaches the judge. "Your Honor," he says, "I will pay this man's fine. I would like to serve his sentence for him as well. If I do this, will you allow him to go free and forgive him of his debt?" The judge considers this man's offer and accepts it. The handcuffs are taken off you and placed upon the wrists of this man. You are now free. Your debt has been paid. As the man is escorted out of the room, you thank him with tears in your eyes. You have never felt such an overwhelming sense of relief—or gratitude.

In the first scenario, you didn't know any of the details of your crime, so you had no idea of the fate you'd been freed from. In the second scenario, however, you were made aware of what you were guilty of and therefore understood *exactly* what you were forgiven for. The details didn't change. It was only your *awareness* of the details that changed. But by having become aware of the full gravity of your situation, you were much more thankful for the final result. When you were aware of no more than simply being forgiven but had no idea what you were being forgiven for, your thankfulness was fleeting at best.

Likewise, if you don't understand exactly what you have been (or still need to be) saved from, you will only see Jesus as something you add to your life to make it better. You will see Him as the cream in your coffee rather than the air in your lungs. He will be something you add to your life to make it better, not your entire source of life. And if you view Jesus in this way, as soon as life gets hard, you will likely reject Him as yet another solution that did not fulfill its promise of enhancing your life.

If, on the other hand, you recognize how lost and hopeless you truly were apart from Jesus, even the most difficult trials will be unable to turn you back to your old way of living apart from Him.[2] In fact, when these trials cause pain and suffering in your life, you will draw closer to Jesus because of them. This is why it is so necessary to come to a biblical understanding of the dire situation every human being has been born into.

The Problem in All of Us

As much as we all like to think of ourselves as good people, the Bible tells us otherwise. When Adam chose to follow his own path by eating the forbidden fruit, he turned away from God, and sin entered into the hearts of mankind.[3] There are entire books written that explain this reality in much more detail, but the main thing to realize is this: Since that day, this seed of sin has been passed on to everyone who has ever lived (with one exception, which we'll discuss later). Every person, no matter how good they believe themselves to be, has been born with sin in their heart and is therefore separated from God.

We are All Guilty of Sin

The Bible tells us that "*all* have sinned and fall short of the glory of God."[4] That verse alone sums up our plight pretty clearly, but let's talk through a few scenarios. For instance, in the Ten Commandments we are commanded not to steal.[5] Have you ever stolen anything, even something small? What about when you were a child? If your answer is yes, then you are a thief. *Wait a second! I'm not a thief just because I stole a candy from the corner store when I was five!* Okay, how many times do you need to steal something before you are a thief? Ten? Twenty? A hundred? Even if you only stole something one time, you now qualify as a thief.

Let's take a look at another commandment: You shall not lie.[6] Have you ever told a lie? Of course you have. We all have. So again, how many lies does it take to be a liar? I hate to break it to you, but you are a liar. *But these are just little things. They can't matter. I still haven't broken any of the major laws.* Are you sure about that?

---

2 Romans 5:3–5.
3 Romans 5:18.
4 Romans 3:23.
5 Exodus 20:15.
6 Exodus 20:16.

Most people would consider the command to not commit adultery as one of the "major" commandments, so let's start there.[7] Have you ever had sex with a woman who is not your wife? Before you claim to have fulfilled this command faithfully, we need to look at the words of Jesus as He unpacks this commandment further:

> You have heard the commandment that says, "You must not commit adultery. But I say, anyone who even looks at a woman with lust has already committed adultery with her in his heart (Matthew 5:27–28).

I probably don't need to point out that you are reading a book about pornography for you to see how this verse more than likely applies to you. But lets give you the benefit of the doubt and say you are reading this book for a friend and can honestly say you have never even looked upon a woman lustfully. Even if that were the case, you would still have to admit to the lying and stealing. The reality is, if you have broken even *one* of God's laws, you are guilty of breaking *all* of them.[8] You are no longer perfect.

So, based on this knowledge, are you innocent or guilty? Every one of us, if we are being honest, must admit we are guilty of sin. Which brings us to the next question: Are we still in good standing with God?

We are All Separated from God Because of Our Sin

Based on what we just looked at, do you think you will spend eternity in heaven or in hell?

If you are like most people, you will say heaven, even after acknowledging that you are guilty of sin. Why is this? Most people, when pressed for an explanation, will answer with something along the lines of "Because God is good, He will overlook my sin and let me into heaven." Imagine if you tried that same logic in a court of law. What would happen if, after being found guilty, you approached the judge and told him you are appealing to his goodness as a loving man to ignore your crime and let you off the hook. He would tell you it's *because* of his goodness that he must punish you for

---

7 Exodus 20:14.

8 James 2:10.

your crime. Letting a guilty man go free would not be just—it would be unjust. It would be the opposite of goodness.

In the same way, *because* God is good, He *cannot* excuse your sin. If He were to begin accepting liars, thieves, adulterers, and other sinners into heaven, He would be compromising His goodness and holiness, which would be against His very nature. As a loving and just God, He *must* have righteous anger toward anything that is unholy and hurtful toward those He loves.

But what if someone doesn't even know they are sinning? The Bible tells us that the law of God is written on the hearts of men.[9] This is why all people understand right and wrong universally. Everyone, no matter what culture or religion they are a part of, knows that certain things—lying, cheating, stealing, murder—are wrong. Some people will go to great lengths to justify their behavior, but ultimately they know it's wrong. And, just like in our legal system, ignorance of the law is not an excuse for breaking the law. But the bottom line is, you no longer fall into this category. You know full well that you are a sinner. So this argument can no longer justify you because it no longer applies to you.

I know this message of judgment, hell, and eternal punishment is not popular in our culture today. But society doesn't determine our eternal fate, God does. And as much as we want to reject this reality, the Bible is very clear about how He views sinners:

> The Lord observed the extent of human wickedness on the earth, and he saw that everything they thought or imagined was consistently and totally evil (Genesis 6:5).
>
> The human heart is the most deceitful of all things, and desperately wicked. Who really knows how bad it is? (Jeremiah 17:9),
>
> Because you are stubborn and refuse to turn from your sin, you are storing up terrible punishment for yourself. For a day of anger is coming, when God's righteous judgment will be revealed (Romans 2:5).

---

9 Romans 2:15.

> All of us used to live that way, following the passionate desires and inclinations of our sinful nature. By our very nature we were subject to God's anger, just like everyone else (Ephesians 2:3).

The Bible is clear that we are *all* guilty of sin, and the consequence of our guilt is eternal separation from God. So it appears that we must somehow become righteous and acceptable again. But there's nothing we can do to make ourselves right in His eyes. We've already disqualified ourselves through our imperfection. Does this mean we are destined to spend eternity separated from God in the fires of hell?

No, this painful reality breaks God's heart even more than it breaks yours. Because of His great love, He has provided a solution to this problem that is available to every one of us.

The Solution to Our Separation

In order for us to understand the *true* solution to this problem, we need to recognize and expose the *false* solution that so many people have been placing their hope in. Many people today, including a large amount of those who claim to be followers of Jesus, believe the only way to be made right with God is to regain His favor through enough good behavior. They believe the path to becoming a "good" person is to do a "good" job of following God's rules. This false view of the gospel is why so many people believe the Bible to be nothing more than a book of restrictive rules devoid of any life-changing power. This is why we need to look at the original purpose of these rules—commonly referred to as *the law*—if we want to understand the true message of the gospel.

The Purpose of The Law

The purpose of the law (God's rules) is not to show you how to earn your own salvation. In fact, it's supposed to do the exact opposite. The purpose of the law is to make you fully aware of your *inability* to earn your own salvation. Imagine you see a plain cardboard box sitting on the bookshelf at a friend's house. You probably wouldn't think anything of it. Now imagine if the box had a sign on it that said, "DO NOT LOOK IN THIS

BOX UNDER ANY CIRCUMSTANCES!" What do you want to do? If you're like me, you will become obsessed with knowing what's in that box. You *have* to know! After all, if it's that big of a secret, it must be something cool. This illustrates the purpose of the law at work in your life. It exposes—and even arouses—the sin within you so you can become aware of your inability to control it.

> It was the law that showed me my sin. I would never have known that coveting is wrong if the law had not said, "You must not covet." But sin used this command to arouse all kinds of covetous desires within me! If there were no law, sin would not have that power (Romans 7:7–8).

The law makes us aware of God's requirements but fails to give us the power to live up to them. In fact, our awareness of the law actually makes it harder for us to live up to them. For example, let's look at the temptation of pornography. You know it's wrong to look at porn because lusting is a violation of God's law. But what happens in your mind if you start focusing on trying to avoid pornography? If you are like most men, even thinking about *avoiding* porn causes you to think about porn all the more. It brings the temptation to the front of your mind. For me, just typing this paragraph right now is causing some old memories to resurface, which is exactly what Paul was talking about with coveting in the previous verse. Coveting became a temptation for him only after he found out it was wrong and tried to control it.

Paul also shows us how the law is the great equalizer, condemning us all equally:

> [The law's] purpose is to keep people from having excuses, and to show that the *entire world* is guilty before God. For no one can ever be made right with God by doing what the law commands. The law simply shows us how sinful we are (Romans 3:19–20).

The law levels the playing field, takes away any excuse, discredits every attempt at justification, and shows the entire world how guilty we all are. The law outlines, in full detail, the standard of holiness required by God and allows us to understand how short we fall. It removes any sense of "good" or "bad" and places everyone in the category of "guilty."

If this all seems hopeless to you—the opposite of good news—you are correct. This is terrible news. But God knew when He gave the law to man no one would ever be able to fulfill it. Remember, He didn't give us the law in order for us to keep it; He gave us the law to bring us to our knees in hopelessness so we could recognize our need for a Savior. The ultimate purpose of the law is to point us to the Cross of Christ. By understanding the hopelessness of this reality we are born into, we can now fully appreciate how great the gift of God's grace and salvation truly is.

This is also why the gospel is so offensive to people who are still separated from God. Nobody likes being told they aren't good enough. Until you recognize your need for a Savior, all you will hear in the gospel message is that you are broken...you can't fix yourself...you will never be good enough. What it all comes down to, though, is the difference between viewing yourself through the lens of pride and the lens of humility. God wants us to become humbled and admit that we will never be good enough to save ourselves. He wants us to recognize our need to be rescued and reach out for help. If you never admit to your need for help in your life, you will continue to buy into the lie that you can someday be good enough to save yourself. Whether you say it outright or not, you are essentially claiming you can be good enough to overcome your need for Jesus. And when you say it that way, it's easier to recognize this belief for what it really is—pride. This is exactly why God opposes the proud but gives grace to the humble.[10]

God Is Opposed to the Proud...

If we look at our salvation while maintaining a prideful view of ourselves, we will naturally believe we can follow the rules well enough to earn our ticket to heaven. This is the basic message behind the majority of world religions. Whether it's Islam, Buddhism, Hinduism, Judaism, or any of the others, the message tends to be the same: Maintain a certain level of

10 James 4:6.

morality and you will earn the right to go to a better place when you die. But as long as you still believe that you can save yourself through good behavior, you won't look outside of yourself for answers. Pride—especially religious pride—keeps people from seeing their need for Jesus.

If you don't believe that God doesn't want you to try and save yourself through following the rules, take a look at what Jesus had to say to the religious-rule-keeping all-stars of His day, the Pharisees:

> What sorrow awaits you teachers of religious law and you Pharisees. Hypocrites! For you shut the door of the Kingdom of Heaven in people's faces. You won't go in yourselves, and you don't let others enter either (Matthew 23:13).

> What sorrow awaits you teachers of religious law and you Pharisees. Hypocrites! For you are so careful to clean the outside of the cup and the dish, but inside you are filthy—full of greed and self-indulgence! (Matthew 23:25).

> What sorrow awaits you teachers of religious law and you Pharisees. Hypocrites! For you are like whitewashed tombs—beautiful on the outside but filled on the inside with dead people's bones and all sorts of impurity (Matthew 23:27).

If anyone were ever going to be saved by keeping the law, it would have been these guys. But Jesus was constantly opposing these prideful men and showing them that no matter how hard they tried to keep the rules, their hearts remained full of sin. They were looking at salvation as an outside-in transformation (change your behavior and then your heart will change). But God *always* works from the inside out. John Eldredge explains this wonderfully in his book, *The Utter Relief of Holiness*:

> I would love to have heard his tone of voice, seen the expression on his face. I think we can be fairly confident that when Jesus thundered, "Woe to you," everyone just about peed their pants. And what is the issue here? Shallow holiness. Faking it. Ignoring the deeper issues of the soul. As far as Jesus is concerned,

> holiness is a matter of the heart. "Clean the inside of the cup and dish, and the outside will be cleaned as well." The model of personal transformation that [Jesus] offers is internal to external. It's a transformation of the heart, the mind, the will, the soul—which then begins to express itself externally in our actions. This is absolutely critical in order to understand Jesus and his genuine goodness.[11]

The Pharisees knew deep down they weren't *really* fulfilling all the requirements of the law. They were merely faking perfection in order to appear as if their rules-based path to salvation really did have the power to change their hearts.

It's the same with us today, isn't it? If your hope for salvation is based on your behavior, you will always know deep down that it isn't working. You will spend your energy trying to at least appear better than others in order to claim some sort of forward spiritual progress in your life. But this knowledge of not being able to be a good enough person will cause shame to well up within you. Once again, this hiddenness, deception, and shame will create the perfect environment for pornography to grab hold of you and drag you deeper into its trap. So, the very thing you are doing to earn favor in God's eyes—trying to be good enough—is actually arousing more sin within you. And, on top of that, it is also keeping you from recognizing the only thing that ever *will* make you right in God's eyes—the Cross of Jesus.

> Rome is burning, Jesus says. Drop your fiddle, change your life and come to Me. Let go of the good days that never were—a regimented church you never attended, traditional virtues you never practiced, legalistic obedience you never honored, and a sterile orthodoxy you never accepted. The old era is done. The decisive inbreak of God has happened.[12]

---

11 John Eldredge, *The Utter Relief of Holiness* (New York: Hachette Book Group, 2013).

12 Brennan Manning, *The Ragamuffin Gospel* (Colorado Springs: Multnomah Books, 1990), 108.

...but Gives Grace to the Humble

It's easy for us to recognize we aren't perfect, but we often don't see how deep the problem truly is until we come to a complete loss of hope in our own resources. This is why many men need to reach rock bottom before they are willing to even consider their need for a Savior. I had to recognize that my sinfulness was destroying the heart of my wife before I was willing to accept how messed up I truly was. I had to realize that my problem wasn't just a few specific sins within me, but a heart that was completely dead because of sin. I had to stop trying to overcome my sin through prideful self-righteousness and reach out to God for mercy, just like the tax collector in Luke 18:

> Two men went to the Temple to pray. One was a Pharisee, and the other was a despised tax collector. The Pharisee stood by himself and prayed this prayer: "I thank you, God, that I am not a sinner like everyone else. For I don't cheat, I don't sin, and I don't commit adultery. I'm certainly not like that tax collector! I fast twice a week, and I give you a tenth of my income."
>
> But the tax collector stood at a distance and dared not even lift his eyes to heaven as he prayed. Instead, he beat his chest in sorrow, saying, "O God, be merciful to me, for I am a sinner." I tell you, this sinner, not the Pharisee, returned home justified before God. For those who exalt themselves will be humbled, and those who humble themselves will be exalted (Luke 18:10–13).

When I came to understand the full scope of my sin and recognized how powerless I was to fix it, I was finally humbled before God. And because of His grace, even though I was still very much a sinner, He sent His Son Jesus to pay my penalty and make me righteous in His sight.

This is the beauty of God's grace. It's His free gift of salvation, love, and acceptance—regardless of whether you deserve it or not. Despite your unworthiness to receive His favor, He still chose to sacrifice His only Son in order to pay the full penalty of your sin, providing the way for you to become acceptable in His sight and making it possible for you to spend eternity with Him.[13] The Cross of Jesus was God's rescue mission to save *you*. And it's not because of anything you have done; it's a gift given purely out of His love. The only requirement for you to receive this gift of salvation is to humble yourself before Him and admit how much you need it. You must realize that your résumé, no matter how impressive it may be, is worthless compared to what Christ has done for you on the cross:

> I [Paul] once thought these things [his religious résumé] were valuable, but now I consider them worthless because of what Christ has done. Yes, everything else is worthless when compared with the infinite value of knowing Christ Jesus my Lord. For his sake I have discarded everything else, counting it all as garbage, so that I could gain Christ and become one with him. I no longer count on my own righteousness through obeying the law; rather, I become righteous through faith in Christ. For God's way of making us right with himself depends on faith (Philippians 3:7–9).

Paul understood that the only thing powerful enough to overcome the sinful nature within him was faith in Jesus. Yes, it was probably hard at first for him to see his religious education, his meticulous rule keeping, and his devotion to upholding the integrity of Judaism as meaningless, but it was only by humbling himself and recognizing these things for what they were—garbage—that he was finally able to be made righteous through Jesus.

Jesus didn't die for you just to tell you to strive harder and quit sinning. He came to create a way for you to have eternal life even though you *can't* quit sinning. Trusting that the Cross of Christ *alone* has paid your debt *in full* is the only requirement to experience this new life. Once again, it's not a matter of being good enough, because we know God's standard is perfection. The only way you can be made perfect in His eyes is to hand your sin over to Jesus so His blood can pay for all of it, once and for all. Just as the man in the courtroom took your punishment so you could be set free, Jesus paid the penalty of your sin so that you could experience

---

13 Romans 5:8.

eternal life with Him. Salvation is made possible by His work on the cross and what He has done, period. It's the *only* solution to our sin problem. There is no other way.

The Choice is Yours

If you died today and God asked you, "Why should I let you into heaven?" what would your answer be? If your mind goes straight to thoughts such as *I am a good person* or *look at all the great things I have done*, then it shows you are still placing your hope for salvation in your behavior. God will respond to your list of "good things" by telling you they were not good enough to overcome your guilt.[14] If, however, you immediately think, *I am not worthy to be here. I shouldn't be here. But Jesus has paid my way and covered my debt. He has made me righteous. Because of Him, I now have the right to be here,* it shows that you have reached a point of humbling yourself before the cross. It's here, in this position of humility, where you will begin to experience God's amazing grace and all the life, joy, and freedom that comes from fully trusting in Christ.

What it all comes down to is this: There are really only two options in this life. The first is choosing to spend your life attempting to gain God's acceptance by following the law. But if you choose this path, your eternal destination will be based solely on your own goodness and behavior, which can never bring you to a point of perfection. As we saw earlier, you have already disqualified yourself of any hope for perfection through this path. In reality, this option isn't even an option no matter how much you want to believe it is. Choosing this is choosing to remain separated from God. The other option is to accept His gracious gift of salvation through His Son, Jesus. And the only thing you need to do to receive this gift is believe that Jesus truly is Lord, His death has paid for all of your sin, and His resurrection has given you the gift of eternal life.[15]

How Does This Help Me with Porn?

Your pornography addiction may not be the most pressing issue in your

14 Matthew 7:21–23.

15 Romans 10:9; John 3:16.

life right now. Think about it: If you have yet to be reconciled to God, it doesn't matter at all whether you ever get your porn habit under control or not. You may become nothing more than an ex-porn addict who is still destined to spend eternity in hell.

I encourage you to ask yourself, where are you at right now in God's eyes? Have you been made right with Him, or are you still separated from Him because of your guilt as a sinner? If you are tired of striving to save yourself through behavior, realize you have no hope of ever paying your own debt, and recognize your desperate need for a divine rescue, then I encourage you to pray the following prayer:

Father God, I recognize that I am completely powerless to save myself. I understand that no amount of good behavior will ever be able to overcome the sin that is within me. It's because of this reality that I need to be rescued. I need a Savior. I believe in the truth that Jesus took all of my sin upon Himself on the cross and paid my debt in full through His death. I thank you that through His payment, I am now made righteous in your eyes. I also thank you that because of His resurrection, I now have His life within me and will spend eternity in heaven with you. Thank you for your grace, Father. Thank you for loving and accepting me as your child. Amen.

LIE #5

My Pornography Addiction Separates Me from God's Love

Knowing that we can be loved exactly as we are gives us all the best opportunity for growing into the healthiest of people.

FRED ROGERS

Growing up in the Northwest was pretty awesome, especially during summer breaks when I didn't have to waste a large part of each day stuck inside a classroom. I'd spend my summers riding bikes, building forts, playing with Legos, and of course, wasting copious amounts of time in front of the Nintendo. But the one thing I looked forward to the most every summer, without a doubt, was going to Camp Harlow.

A week at Camp Harlow felt like a week in heaven. The camp had a pool (with a water slide), a campfire pit, go-karts, night games, and all the other cool stuff you would expect at a summer camp. The real purpose of Camp Harlow, though, was to teach kids about Jesus. Every year during the final campfire of the week, the camp speaker would invite anyone to come forward to receive Jesus as their Savior. I don't remember going forward every year, but I know I did at least three or four times. I'm not sure what prompted me to feel the need to ask Jesus back into my heart multiple times, but I guess I thought there was a chance He had left me because of my sinfulness. Or perhaps He had never even moved into my heart in the first place.

I'd show up on the first day of camp highly *motivated* to be a good follower of Jesus, which was easy in a setting where everyone else wanted to follow Him as well. As the week went on, the camp speaker would tell us how much we needed Jesus, which made me realize how far I was falling short. This would cause me to feel *condemnation* for not measuring up to God's standards. By the end of the week, I would *rededicate* my life to Jesus, promising Him I would never sin again. Some years, if I felt especially condemned by the amount of sin in my life, I would go so far as to question whether I was even saved at all and would go forward and ask Jesus back into my heart again…just to be safe. I didn't realize it at the time, but I was living out the same cycle during a week at camp that I would live out over and over for the first 30 years of my life. Author Steve McVey calls this the "Motivation-Condemnation-Rededication Cycle," which summed up my approach to religion perfectly.

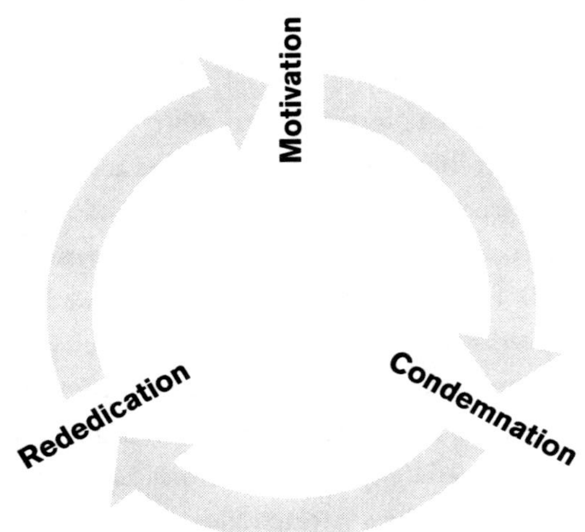

On the surface, this cycle doesn't seem so bad, does it? After all, wasn't it drawing me back to God? Well, no, it actually wasn't. Yes, I would leave camp on a spiritual high, fully desiring to be an amazing "Jesus person" and never sin again. But as soon as I got back to the real world and faced real temptations (like the stack of *Playboys* in my closet), I'd be right back on the same cycle. I would be highly motivated to resist the temptation for a day or two, but inevitably I'd give in, which led to more feelings of condemnation. I'd feel like a failure and believe God was ashamed of me for sinning after I promised Him that I wouldn't. I'd rededicate my life to Him (again) and vow to try even harder this time (again). I promised to read my Bible every day, pray more, and do all the things a good church kid should do. Surely doing these "good" things would bring me back into a close relationship with Him. If that were the case, though, why did it cause me to feel further away from Him?

We tend to see this very same cycle in pornography addiction. Whenever I was done looking at porn, in that moment of postmasturbation clarity, I would become highly motivated to give up porn for good. I'd throw away my stash of magazines. I'd delete any images or videos I'd saved on my computer. I'd close any known loopholes in my filter software. I was done. I was motivated. This time it was going to work. But within a few days, the temptation would return and I would fail. The shame and condemnation would come back by the truckload. *Why am I such a terrible sinner? Why can't I control this? Real followers of Jesus don't struggle with this. Am I really a follower? Am I really saved? God must be so ashamed of me.*

I felt as if He had turned His back on me. I had no idea how to get my pornography addiction under control, so I would once again promise to try harder to manage it, hoping I could somehow earn back God's love and acceptance. I was constantly rededicating myself to a God I believed kept rejecting me because of my sin. So instead of drawing me closer to God, this cycle was actually causing me to pull away from Him.

I always felt the need to clean myself up before I could be close to God. Ultimately, though, the method of cleansing I was attempting was all about what I could do for myself. *I* need to control my sin. *I* need to try harder. *I* need to do something to make myself acceptable again. As we saw in the previous chapter, however, sin isn't something we can control—let alone overcome—apart from Jesus. As long as you keep focusing on fixing your own sin, you will never find true freedom from it.

The only thing that can stop the Motivation-Condemnation-Rededication

Cycle from going on forever is reliance on Jesus to set you free from your sin. Once you begin to understand that God no longer holds any of your sin against you,[1] and that He has already forgiven *all* of your sins at the cross, the feelings of shame and condemnation that keep this cycle spinning will cease. You must come to understand that He isn't looking for what you can do—He's looking for *you!* He wants to be with you. In fact, His desire to be with you is so strong that He sent Jesus to pay your ransom *while you were still a sinner.*[2] If He was willing to sacrifice His own Son to save you when you still wanted nothing to do with Him, why would He turn His back on you now that you actually want to be with Him? That idea doesn't make any sense, because it isn't true. The truth is, all of your sin has been paid for by Jesus, which means it will *never* separate you from God's love or acceptance again.

TRUTH: Your sin will never separate you from God's unconditional love and acceptance.

Just as you cannot earn God's favor with good behavior, you cannot lose His favor with bad behavior. Your salvation—and your daily relationship with God—is all a gift from Him. Your ability to follow the rules, be good enough, or be worthy enough has absolutely nothing to do with it.

> God saved you by his grace when you believed. And you can't take credit for this; it is a gift from God. Salvation is not a reward for the good things we have done, so none of us can boast about it (Ephesians 2:8–9).

This can be hard for us to understand, because it goes against everything in our human nature. We feel like we need to at least contribute *something* to the equation, but all God asks for is faith. The only thing you need to do is believe that what He says is true. If you trust Him, He will give you His unconditional love and acceptance as a gift—no strings attached. It's the most lopsided gift in the history of eternity.

---

1 Romans 8:1.

2 Romans 5:8.

This, my friend, is grace. And God's grace changes everything.

God Saved You by His Grace

The most beautiful word in the Bible, in my opinion, is *grace*. Grace is the disproportionately generous blessing of God given to those who deserve nothing from Him but judgment. It's His unconditional love and acceptance poured out on us solely because of what Jesus has done—not because of anything we have done to earn it. We are so unworthy of God's grace, yet He gives it to us freely and unashamedly. Grace is the good news that more than makes up for all the bad news in this world.

Grace Means You are Loved Unconditionally

When you begin to experience God's grace in your heart, it changes everything. You realize that He isn't waiting for a better, future version of you to love. He loves you as you are *right now* (even if your pants are around your ankles). He doesn't expect you to fix your junk before you come to Him. In fact, He wants you to come to Him *with* your junk so He can fix it for you. He knew all along you would be right where you are today—no matter how messed up you are—and He *still* chose to send Jesus to set you free.

When you come to realize there is nothing you can do to make God stop loving you or pull away from you, it frees you from the fear of not measuring up. As Brennan Manning so eloquently stated:

> The only lasting freedom from self-consciousness comes from a profound awareness that God loves me as I am and not as I should be.[3]

God's unconditional love frees you from viewing Him as distant, judgmental, and angry. It frees you from the shame and condemnation that Satan wants you to heap upon yourself whenever you give in to temptation. It reminds you that it's okay to not be okay.

This may be hard to accept, especially if you have been viewing God as an angry judge looking for an excuse to throw lightning bolts down on you.

---

3 Brennan Manning, *The Ragamuffin Gospel* (Colorado Springs: Multnomah Books, 1990).

You must understand, though, if you are in Christ, that image of an angry God waiting to smite you is yet another lie from Satan meant to keep you from experiencing a fulfilling relationship with the God who loves you to the point of adopting you into His family. The best way to expose and overcome this lie is to look at the truth of Scripture. What does God's Word tell us about how He views us?

There are two sections of Scripture that have transformed my view of God and made His unconditional love come alive in my heart. The first is the story of the lost son in Luke 15, which we looked at in an earlier chapter. The message remains the same: God loves you in the same way a father loves his son. No matter how far you've run from him, He will always be waiting for you with open arms. He won't demand an apology or require you to make amends. He just wants to break out the barbecue and celebrate you coming home to Him.

The second passage is 1 Corinthians 13—a passage I had long been familiar with as "the love chapter" but only recently came to understand as a description of God's love for us as well. God is love,[4] which means any verse describing love is also giving us details about God himself.[5] So with that in mind, take a look at this passage and notice how it describes His love for you:

> Love is patient, love is kind. It does not envy, it does not boast, it is not proud. It does not dishonor others, it is not self-seeking, it is not easily angered, it keeps no record of wrongs. Love does not delight in evil but rejoices with the truth. It always protects, always trusts, always hopes, always perseveres (1 Corinthians 13:4–7).

God is patient and kind with you. He's not easily angered by your sin. In fact, because your sins have all been forgiven through Jesus, He keeps no record of them. And just like the father of the lost son, He will never stop hoping for you to come back to Him.

Nothing will ever be able to separate you from His unfailing love:

---

4 1 John 4:8.

5 Contrary to popular belief, this does not mean love is God.

> I am convinced that nothing can ever separate us from God's love. Neither death nor life, neither angels nor demons, neither our fears for today nor our worries about tomorrow—not even the powers of hell can separate us from God's love (Romans 8:38).

If even demons and death can't separate you from God's love, does it make sense that your sin would be able to? Is your tendency to give in to the desires of your flesh stronger than the powers of hell? I think it's safe to say that *nothing*, not even your struggle with pornography, will ever cause God to stop loving you.

So yes, my friend, God loves you beyond what you could ever imagine, and no amount of sexual sin will ever change that. But as unbelievable as it is to realize the Creator of the universe loves *you* as His adopted son, it gets even better.

Grace Means You are Accepted Unconditionally

At first, there may not appear to be a big difference between being loved and being accepted. It seems like they go hand in hand. If you're like me, though, you may have bought into the lie that just because God *loves* you, it doesn't mean He necessarily *likes* you. We believe that because of what the Bible says, God has to *love* us, but it doesn't mean He has to *accept* us into His "inner circle" of favorite people.

One of my favorite preachers, John Lynch, has a humorous but relevant take on how this often plays out in our minds. Picture God sitting in heaven, watching you as you pray the prayer of salvation we talked about in the last chapter:

> Oh man…he's about to pray the prayer. Not him! I can't stand him! Don't do it! Don't do…GAH! He did it. Fine. You prayed the prayer so I guess I'll let you in. I promised I'd love anyone who trusted my Son so I guess I have to love you. But let's get one thing straight. I DON'T LIKE YOU! I'm only letting you in because I said I would and I'm God so I have to keep my word. I'm going to keep my eye on you though. If you mess up

I'm moving you to the far end of the table. Don't expect me to offer you seconds on dessert. You're lucky you're even here at all.

As ridiculous as that picture may be, sadly, it's how a lot of us believe God views us. But here's the truth: God not only loves you, but He actually likes you. In fact, He's absolutely crazy about you! I can't prove it through Scripture, but I'm pretty sure He brags to the angels about how proud He is of you. And because He loves *all* of His children with *all* of His love, there is no such thing as God's "inner circle" of favorites. If you have put your hope in Christ, you have already been made as acceptable to God as Jesus Himself. Because your acceptance is a product of what Jesus did on the cross—not a product of you earning it—your status as fully acceptable in God's eyes will never change. Not now. Not ever.

I believe there are more people in our churches today, unfortunately, who misunderstand God's grace than have experienced the life change that comes with a proper understanding of it. Countless people are giving up on their faith in Jesus every single day because it doesn't appear to be working for them. They've tried so hard for so long, and yet they still struggle with habitual sin. Life isn't getting any better. They feel like failures.

Many of these well-meaning people eventually lose hope and walk away from God altogether. They start to believe the Bible isn't true because it isn't working for them. But why is this the case? Why isn't the truth of Scripture changing their life?

Maybe it's because the path to salvation they are putting their hope in isn't the true message of the Bible.

Salvation is Not a Reward for the Good Things You Have Done

There are three common views people hold regarding the path to salvation:

- The first view is that we are saved by being good people. We discussed the problems with this view in the previous chapter. Needless to say, you cannot earn your way to heaven through good behavior, so this view can never produce salvation—only empty religion. This was the view of the Pharisees, and Jesus made it clear through His interactions with them that it was not the way to heaven.

- The second view is that we are saved because Jesus paid the penalty for our sins. It's only because of what He did for us on the cross that we are made right in God's eyes. Salvation has nothing to do with our behavior, abilities, or worthiness. In other words, salvation is *not* a reward for the good things we have done, but a *free gift* from God. This message of salvation by grace alone is the true message of the Bible, and the only way anyone can ever be saved.

- The third view, however, is a combination of the first two. It's believing that God's *unconditional* love and acceptance is *conditional* on our ability to keep the rules. (If you think this doesn't make sense, you're correct.) The book of Galatians was written to help the early church recognize and turn away from this false view of the gospel, which is why this view is sometimes referred to as Galatianism. This false view of salvation is unfortunately all too common even to this day. It's a dangerous lie, though, and it will keep you from experiencing the transformed life promised to you in the Scriptures.

The Danger of Galatianism

Many people today believe that their *initial* salvation came from the work of Jesus alone (saved by grace), but they also believe their *continued* salvation—and their acceptance by God—is a reward they maintain only if they are good enough (saved by keeping the law—keeping rules). The problem with this view is, once you require the addition of good behavior to become worthy of receiving grace, it stops being grace. Grace, by definition, is a free gift from God. Once it becomes contingent on anything, it is no longer a gift. It becomes compensation.[6] Likewise, as soon as you

6 Romans 11:6.

create any path for receiving acceptance from God apart from perfection, you are no longer following the law. There is no way to combine being under the law and being under grace without their canceling each other out.

Here's the deeper reality, though: If you don't believe God loves you and accepts you unconditionally because of His grace alone, you aren't believing the true gospel. I know that sounds harsh, but it's the undeniable truth of Scripture. Paul even went so far as to liken this mixed belief system to being under an evil spell:

> Oh, foolish Galatians! Who has cast an evil spell on you? For the meaning of Jesus Christ's death was made as clear to you as if you had seen a picture of his death on the cross. Let me ask you this one question: Did you receive the Holy Spirit by obeying the law of Moses? Of course not! You received the Spirit because you believed the message you heard about Christ. How foolish can you be? After starting your Christian lives in the Spirit, why are you now trying to become perfect by your own human effort? (Galatians 3:1–3).

Did you catch that last part? These early believers knew they had been saved by what Jesus had done for them, but they still went back to the law to try and earn God's favor through their own human effort. But we aren't really that different today. As followers of Jesus, it's easy for us to see how our actions had nothing to do with our salvation. So why is it so hard for us to believe that our actions are just as useless when it comes to our daily acceptance from God after we become saved?

By believing you can contribute to your salvation, you are essentially saying the cross wasn't enough to cover *all* of your sin. You are saying the cross was enough to *get* you saved, but it lacks the power to *keep* you saved. What seems like a humble and righteous motive is actually a sign of pride. You are telling God that your sin is too big for Jesus to cover it and He needs your help to finish the deal.

I had accepted the fact that Jesus had paid for my sin on the cross, but every time I messed up I felt the need to make things right again. I felt I had to earn God's favor back and beg for forgiveness for what I had just done. But think about this: When did Jesus pay for your sins? It was on the cross. And how many of your sins were done *after* the cross? All of them. Every one of your sins—past, present, and even *future* sins—were paid for 2000 years ago when Jesus said, "It is finished." When you accept His payment for your sins, it's for *all* of them. Not just the ones you had committed up to the point of your initial salvation. This idea that we need to keep coming back for forgiveness and make things right every time we sin is the same as telling Jesus we need Him to go back to the cross and do it again.

Let's look at this another way. Imagine you had a credit card with a $50,000 balance on it. If someone came along and paid the full balance for you, would you keep making payments on the card? Of course not. But this is what we are doing with Jesus when we buy into the trap of Galatianism. He paid the full balance of *every* sin in your *entire* life at the cross, but we are still trying to make payments on a balance that no longer exists.

You may be surprised to realize how often the Bible warns us to avoid falling into this trap:

> Once the law points you to Jesus, its job is done. It has no more bearing on your life (Galatians 3:25).

> Christ has truly set us free. Now make sure you stay free, and don't get tied up again in slavery to the law (Galatians 5:1).

> You have died with Christ, and he has set you free from the spiritual powers of this world. So why do you keep on following the rules of the world, such as, "Don't handle! Don't taste! Don't touch!"? Such rules are mere human teachings about things that deteriorate as we use them. These rules may seem wise because they require strong devotion, pious self-denial, and severe bodily discipline. But they provide no help in conquering a person's evil desires (Colossians 2:20–23).

By putting yourself back under the law, you are rejecting God's grace. When you try to be good enough through keeping the rules, you are actually choosing to return to slavery. You are placing an imaginary wall of unachievable morality between you and Jesus. He is your only hope of freedom. This is why it is so important to understand how your behavior—no matter how sinful it may be—can never separate you from God's love or acceptance once you have put your hope in the work of Christ.

Does Grace Give You a Free Pass to Sin?

If our behavior doesn't affect our acceptance, does that mean we can just go off and sin all we want and still be saved? Apparently God really does know everything, because He anticipated this question and inspired Paul to address it directly:

> Should we keep on sinning so that God can show us more and more of his wonderful grace? Of course not! Since we have died to sin, how can we continue to live in it? (Romans 6:1–2).

We know God's grace is proof that we are loved and accepted unconditionally, but did you know it is also proof of your sin nature being dead as well? Grace confirms that we have *already* been made righteous in God's eyes. If you trust that you are under His grace, you must also trust that you are dead to sin. You must trust that your sinful nature really was crucified with Christ, because God cannot accept anyone into His presence if they are still alive to sin. So, as Paul says in the previous verse, if we are dead to sin, how can we continue to walk in it? In other words, sin has no more power over you, so why would you ever choose to go back to it?

Author Bob George used to share this wonderful illustration on his radio show. Imagine you are the owner of a fancy all-you-can-eat restaurant. One day, as you are walking to work, you see a homeless man eating rotten food scraps out of a dumpster. Filled with compassion, you invite him to come into your restaurant and help himself to whatever he wants. You show him all the wonderful food—steak, potatoes, pizza, even a soft-serve ice cream machine with all the toppings—and hand him a plate. Imagine your shock if he were to walk out the back door and start filling the plate with scraps from the dumpster again.

As ridiculous as that would be, it's really no different than someone choosing to go back to a life of sin after they've experienced new life living under God's grace. Once you've been set free from a life of dumpster diving and tasted the buffet of God's grace in your life, you'll see sin for what it really is and it will no longer be appealing to you.

Or, as Solomon so eloquently states in the book of Proverbs:

> As a dog returns to its vomit, so a fool repeats his foolishness (Proverbs 26:11).

As long as you are still viewing God as an angry judge, you won't want to be close to Him. If, however, you come to see Him as a loving Father who accepts you no matter what, you will want to spend time with Him out of desire rather than duty. Not only that, but you will want to do things to please Him, not take advantage of Him.

Think of it this way: Imagine your wife told you she loved you so much she would be willing to forgive you of anything—no matter what—and it would never cause her to reject you or stop loving you. Would you respond by constantly sinning against her and taking advantage of her goodness? Of course not. Her unconditional acceptance of you would cause you to desire to know her, be with her, love her, and serve her all the more.

We naturally want to be with people who love and accept us, and our relationship with God is no different. When you experience His grace, you will draw near to Him in your time of need rather than pull away from Him out of fear or shame.

So yes, under the new covenant of grace, you can sin all you want. You just won't want to.

Shouldn't We Be Taking Our Sin More Seriously?

It may seem like you are taking your sin seriously by working on it, but in reality, you are minimizing it. You are showing that you believe your sin isn't a big problem, and you can handle it just fine on your own. When we approach our sin in this way, we're acting like the Black Knight from *Monty Python and the Holy Grail.* We keep going back into battle only to lose another limb. Instead of accepting the reality that we are outmatched, we continue to taunt sin and act like we're the one winning the battle.

The only way to truly take your sin seriously is to admit the full depth of its power over you. You must recognize your need for God to deal with it for you. By handing your sin over to Him, you are trusting in His power to set you free from it.

Imagine some evil villain coming after you to destroy you. Who would you want on your side to protect you: Bruce Banner or the Hulk? If you are taking the threat seriously, you call in the Hulk to smash the crap out of your enemy. But by choosing to fight sin on your own and not handing it over to God, you're sending in Bruce Banner. And that's not going to end well.

God's grace is the only thing strong enough to give you the power and motivation to truly overcome sin.

In Christ, We Can Do Good Things

A lot of people reject the idea of salvation by grace alone because the Bible is very clear that we need to be doing good works for Christ. James tells us our faith is dead if it isn't producing good works.[7] But the question isn't whether or not we should be doing good things for God. The question is, what's your motivation for doing those good things? Are you doing them to try and earn God's favor, or are you doing them because they are the natural outflow of a heart made alive through Christ?

I know I sound like a broken record, but here it is again: Good works can never earn God's favor. You cannot, and did not, earn your salvation by following the law.

But does that mean the rules of the law no longer apply to you if you are in Christ? Well, yes and no. We first need to consider three other points in order to understand exactly how good works fit in to a life lived under grace.

1. What is Your Responsibility?

First, we need to define what a law is. A law is a specific rule with an attached consequence. Take, for instance, the speed limit. The law says you can only drive 65 on the freeway. If you exceed the speed limit law, you

---

7 James 2:20.

will receive a consequence, which will likely be a ticket. If, however, you are given an exemption that releases you from the penalty of the law, does it suddenly mean you *should* drive 100 through a school zone? Just because the consequence is no longer attached to the law doesn't mean it's wise to completely ignore the wisdom behind the law.

Likewise, we know there is no longer any condemnation for those who are in Christ. The penalty of death that comes with breaking God's law has already been paid for you. But God is the same today as He was when He first gave the law to man, which means His morality hasn't changed. Even though we are no longer under the *penalty* of the law, the *morality* of the law is still applicable to us.

2. What is Your Motivation?

Next, we need to be aware of the motivation behind our good works. We don't follow the morality of the law in order to earn God's love or acceptance; we do it out of our love for Him and our love for others:

> You have been called to live in freedom, my brothers and sisters. But don't use your freedom to satisfy your sinful nature. Instead, use your freedom to serve one another in love. For the whole law can be summed up in this one command: "Love your neighbor as yourself" (Galatians 5:13–14).

You've been set free from the law by grace, but don't use this freedom as an excuse to sin, use it to love and serve others! The reality is, you aren't under the law, but you *are* under a new commandment:

> Now I am giving you a new commandment: Love each other. Just as I have loved you, you should love each other (John 13:34).

Jesus gave us a new commandment, which is to love others in the same way He has loved us—unconditionally. I've heard some pastors say that this verse means we are no longer under the Ten Commandments. Now, I'm not going to pretend to be smart enough to tell you whether the usage of the word "new" here means an additional commandment, or a commandment that replaces all of the others. What I can tell you, though, is it really doesn't matter. If you are loving God and loving others with the love of Christ, you will be keeping all of the Ten Commandments as part of that.

> Love does no wrong to others, so love fulfills the requirements of the law (Romans 13:10).

The more you understand God's grace, the more you will be able to offer it to others. The more you experience His unconditional love, the more it will flow out of you. You won't be able to hold it back. As Bob Goff says, you will leak Jesus all over everyone you come in contact with. Keeping the morality of the law will happen naturally in your life as you grow closer and closer to Jesus.

3. What is the Source of Your Ability?

Finally, we need to understand the true source behind our good works. It is not us producing any of these good works, but Christ working through us. Whenever I see fruit in my life, I need to remind myself it is not the fruit of Steve, it is the fruit of the Spirit.[8] It is only because of Christ within me that I can do anything good for the Kingdom of God.

This truth became much easier to see once I learned the difference between the *laws* of the Old Testament and the *commissions* of the New Testament epistles.[9] The laws of the Old Testament are telling us, "You must do this or else there will be punishment." The *commissions* of the New Testament are telling us, "Because of the power of Christ within you, this is how you get to act now." See the difference? The New Testament isn't a bunch of additional rules and commands telling us how to live a good life for Jesus. It's telling us who we are now that we are in Christ. The New Testament is telling us what it will look like when we let Jesus live His life through us.

I encourage you to do your own study of this. Any time you find what

---

8 Galatians 5:22–23.

9 I mention the epistles specifically because this concept doesn't apply to the Gospels. The Gospels take place before the resurrection of Christ, which means Jesus was speaking to those who were still under the law. The epistles, however, are postresurrection letters written to those who are "in Christ" and living by the power of the Spirit. This difference between the Gospels and epistles, and what it means for believers, is explained well in Bob George, *Jesus Changes Everything* (Eugene, OR: Harvest House Publishers, 2013).

appears to be a command in the New Testament epistles, look for an "in Christ" statement nearby. I've found it's always close by. For example, look at the following verse from 1 Corinthians:

> Flee from sexual immorality. All other sins a person commits are outside the body, but whoever sins sexually, sins against their own body (1 Corinthians 6:18).

How many times have you read that as a command telling you to resist sexual temptation by your own power? But look at the two verses immediately following:

> Do you not know that your bodies are temples of *the Holy Spirit, who is in you,* whom you have received from God? You are not your own; you were bought at a price. Therefore honor God with your bodies (1 Corinthians 6:19–20).

The church in Corinth didn't fall back into sexual immorality because they were too weak to resist temptation. It was because they had forgotten who they were in Christ. They forgot they had the power of the Holy Spirit living within them. So instead of telling them to shape up and knock off their bad behavior, Paul simply reminds them to remember who they are now that they are in Christ. Likewise, if you are struggling with sexual immorality, it's not because you are still a slave to sin, it's because you have forgotten who you are in Christ. If you can remember that He now lives within you, you can rely on Him to give you the power to honor God with your body.

Paul later shares his own experience of coming to see how this worked in his life:

> What actually took place is this: I tried keeping rules and working my head off to please God, and it didn't work. So I quit being a "law man" so that I could be God's man. Christ's life showed me how, and enabled me to do it. I identified myself completely with him. Indeed, I have been crucified with Christ. My ego is no longer central. It is no longer important that I appear

> righteous before you or have your good opinion, and I am no longer driven to impress God. Christ lives in me. The life you see me living is not "mine," but it is lived by faith in the Son of God, who loved me and gave himself for me (Galatians 2:19 MSG).

Paul stopped trying to please God through good behavior and gave up control of his own life. His service for God was no longer about keeping the rules to try to please Him—it was all about simply trusting Him.

How Will I Know What to Do Without the Rules?

If you've lived your entire life with set rules defining appropriate behavior for you, it can be intimidating to let go of those boundaries. Although living without clearly defined rules may seem like going back to the Wild West, it will not be that way. A life lived by the power of Christ alone is not a life devoid of structure or boundaries. Far from it. It's simply recognizing that you are under a new system now that Christ has fulfilled the law:

> This is the new covenant I will make
> with the people of Israel on that day, says the LORD:
> I will put my laws in their minds,
> and I will write them on their hearts.
> I will be their God,
> and they will be my people (Hebrews 8:10).

We no longer need to go to the written law of the Old Testament to find out how to live because the Holy Spirit is living inside of us. He will let us know what God's will for us is in each moment. Ultimately, this is what it means to be led by the Spirit and to have the law of God written on your heart. Some people call this your conscience or intuition, but the Bible tells us it's much more than that. It's the Spirit of Christ—God Himself—inside of you leading you in how to live your life.

Instead of laws and condemnation, we now have leadings and loving conviction. We no longer have the relationship of a judge and criminal, but a relationship that more closely reflects a parent and child. If there is a particular decision God wants you to make, He will move your thoughts and desires toward it. You will feel a nudge in a certain direction, much like a Father's hand on his child's shoulder.

Likewise, when we forget who we are in Christ and walk back into sin, God comes alongside us as a loving Father to help pick us up and dust us off. It's as if He sits down next to us and says, "Here's what you did. We both know it was wrong. But I still love you. This sin does not define you. It doesn't change how I see you. Let's see what we can learn from this. Let's work on it together." There's no shaming or condemnation, just love and grace. Instead of punishment, it becomes a teaching moment that draws you closer together. When you experience these interactions with God, you no longer feel the need to hide your sin or try to get away with things because you can see how He only wants what's best for you.

The best description I've heard illustrating the difference between trying to control your behavior through the law and controlling it through grace is the example of a city dog and a country dog. Imagine a city dog that is kept in a fenced yard all the time. What happens as soon as the gate is left unlocked? He bolts! The minute he gets an opportunity to break out of the constraints of his fence he goes for it. On the other hand, consider the farm dog that has no fences. He has the freedom to run and explore wherever he wants. But what does he do? He lies down on the front porch of the farmhouse. He knows the world is open to him, but he also knows where to find love and where he will get his needs met. Why would he run away when he's being so well taken care of?

It's the same way with our sin. If we are trying to control it by putting up fences and creating rules, we will break through the gate at the first opportunity. But if we come to see how a life lived under the grace of God is the only way we will ever find fulfillment, a wide-open gate won't even be a temptation.

Yes, you are called to be doing good things for God, but not in order to please Him, and not through your own power. It's the presence of Jesus within you that will enable you to do these good works. And because these works are being done with the proper motive—loving others with His love—these works will actually please God.

How Does This Help Me with Porn?

This is *the* truth that has the potential to change everything for you. A proper understanding of God's grace is the only thing that can ever set you free from the Motivation-Condemnation-Rededication Cycle. Likewise, a misunderstanding of God's grace has the potential to keep you from experiencing true freedom from the bondage of sin in your life.

Before I understood what it meant to be under God's grace, I would feel immense shame every time I gave in to the temptation to look at porn. Instead of running to Him to help me overcome my sin, I would pull away from Him and hide. I kept trying to fix my sinfulness on my own, which kept me from running back to Him—my only hope of overcoming sin at all.

But now I know that God doesn't turn His back on me when I fall. I know my sin can never separate me from Him. This understanding of His grace allows me to come to Him in thankfulness rather than hiding from Him in shame. Instead of running away, I now run to Him.

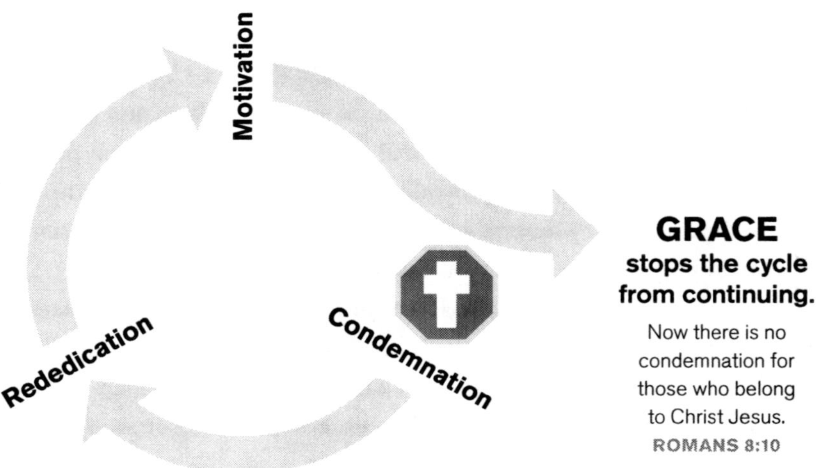

Learning to respond to my sin in this way was a major step in my journey to freedom from my porn addiction. When you come to God in thankfulness and recognize how His grace covers all your sin—especially the sin you just committed—it does three very important things:

1. It puts your focus back on God, which allows you to seek recovery by His power and not your own. When I was still trying to fix my own sin, my mind remained obsessed with my sinfulness. All I saw were my failed attempts to overcome it.

2. Responding to your sin in this way stops the Motivation-Condemnation-Rededication Cycle. You no longer feel the need to move from motivation to condemnation, because God's grace removes all condemnation. And because your motivation is now to simply trust God rather than trying to earn His favor, you no longer have to rely on your own abilities to keep you moving forward. You can rest, knowing that His unlimited power and resources will sustain you.

3. Lastly, this response to sin is a major victory in spiritual warfare. Satan is no fool. If he sees your sin ultimately drawing you closer to God, he's going to focus his efforts elsewhere. He's not going to keep tempting you in the same area if he realizes that it's providing opportunities for you to grow closer to Christ.

Once you are in Christ, your sin—even your pornography habit—will never be able to separate you from the love of God. No matter how badly you've screwed up, His grace is big enough to cover it. He will always love you and accept you unconditionally. And even though this sounds like a license to sin all you want, it's actually the truth that sets you free from the bondage of habitual sin.

So remember, God doesn't invite you into His family because of what you can do. He invites you in because He wants to be with you. The God who created the entire universe wants a close relationship with *you*.

> What does He want from us? He just wants *us*. Not our promises. Not our good intentions. Not even our [religious] service. Everything else takes care of itself when we just rest in His arms, allowing Him to act through us. What a joy and a relief. It isn't a passive lifestyle, but a peaceful one where we actively

rest in Him and He does it all. It is a walk of grace—and it really is amazing![10]

God's grace really is amazing.

Father, thank you that my sin no longer separates me from you because Jesus already paid the price for it on the cross. Thank you that you love me in spite of my failures—even the ones I have yet to commit—and that your acceptance of me will never change. Thank you that you see me as righteous and holy because of Jesus in me. Please live your life through me as you have promised to do. I cannot live this life without you.

10 Steve McVey, *Grace Walk* (Eugene, OR: Harvest House Publishers, 2005), 175.

LIE #6

I'm Strong Enough to Control My Pornography Addiction on My Own

If you can't control your peanut butter, you can't expect to control your life.

BILL WATTERSON

I'm a control freak. I'd much rather do something on my own than take the time to show someone else how to do it. They might mess it up or make a mistake, and then I'd need to just do it myself anyway. I like to think I act this way because I'm a take-charge type of guy with strong leadership skills. In reality, I don't like to give up control, and it's often because I'm afraid of trusting others.

I am not proud of this. Which is why I'm working so hard to control my desire for being in control. (See what I did there?)

I've always been this way. When my parents used to take my brother and me to the go-kart track as kids, we always had two options. We could drive the little kiddie-karts around the track on our own (which would probably get passed by an electric Wal-Mart scooter), or we could ride shotgun with my dad as he drove a *real* go-kart. These things were crazy fast, cornered on a dime, and probably ran on rocket fuel. Everything in me wanted to drive the real go-karts, but in order to qualify, you needed to have a state-issued driver's license. So what did I do? I drove the kiddie-kart. I didn't want to be a passenger. I wanted to be in control.

For years, I believed I was doing a good job of controlling my life. But there was always one thing I just couldn't get under control—my pornography addiction. No matter how hard I tried to control my wayward sexuality, I always felt like it controlled me.

Believe me, I tried everything to control it. Sometimes I'd do great for a week or two, but as soon as I began to think I was getting my sin under control, I'd immediately fall. No matter what I tried, nothing worked for long.

So I kept looking for new answers. I looked for new books to tell me what I needed to do to overcome this terrible habit. I looked for new sermons that would give me the steps I needed to take to get free. I searched everywhere for the missing secret of how I could effectively control my sin, but I never found it.

I was asking the wrong question, though.

I kept asking, "What do *I* need to do to control my sin?" But the reality is, there was nothing *I* could do. I *couldn't* win this fight with my own power. If I were ever going to find freedom from my pornography addiction, I would need to look outside of myself for the answer.

TRUTH: In order to find true freedom, you must give up on your own ability to control your sin.

The only way any of us will ever find lasting freedom from our pornography habit—or any sin for that matter—is to reach out to Jesus for help. You simply aren't strong enough to fight sin on your own. None of us are. That's because all sin is a spiritual battle with a very real adversary who will choke you out if you try to fight him one-on-one. But remember, greater is He that is in you than He that is in the world.[1] So if you're trusting in the superior power of Jesus to help win the battle for you, your victory has already been won.

1 1 John 4:4.

It isn't easy for us to accept this. We don't want to admit we need help. Heck, we don't even like asking for directions. There's something in us as men that makes us want to fight our battles solo—especially these deeply personal battles. We want to believe we are strong enough to control our sin on our own. We all want to be a spiritual Rambo.

If you're being honest with yourself, though, being told you can't control your sin probably isn't that big of a shock to you. The fact that you're reading this book means you are already beginning to explore your need for outside help. But what happens if you're at the point where you recognize that you keep failing but you aren't ready to reach out to Jesus yet?

Chances are, you will keep finding ways to justify your sin—or make excuses for it—until you figure out how to finally get it under control.

You will also be extremely tempted to keep your sin hidden no matter what, which will require you to become an expert at lying to cover your tracks, manipulating others to get your way, and digging yourself out of any mess you end up in. Because you lied to your wife and she believed you the previous ten times, you assume you will be able to do it again and again. Since you've successfully hidden your online behavior for years now, you become extremely confident that no one will find out what you've been up to. These deceitful tactics seem to work well at first, so you'll continue to repeat them to keep from being exposed. Eventually, you will start to believe there is no situation too difficult for you to wiggle out of.

If you continue down this path long enough, you will more than likely come to view yourself as invincible. You may still recognize you aren't doing very well at controlling your sin, but at least you are doing a great job of managing its effect on your life. The longer you believe that lie, the harder it will be for you to recognize your need for outside help. Which is why everything in your life may appear to be manageable for you right now. But eventually, God will lovingly step in and allow all the hidden crap in your life to hit the fan.

This was exactly the experience I had in my own life. Even though I asked God for His help with my sin on occasion, my actions were telling Him I didn't actually want Him to interfere. I continued to use dishonesty and manipulation to control the effects of my sin rather than handling things His way. I was telling Him I could manage my life just fine on my own.

But He loved me too much to sit back and watch me destroy myself. He wasn't going to allow me to keep wandering into battles I couldn't win. He knew my desire for control was hindering me from knowing Him fully and personally. That's why He never stopped pursuing me, or stripping away anything that gave me a false sense of control in my life. He graciously allowed me to reach the end of my rope, where I could finally see how incapable I was to control my sin on my own. He brought me to a point where I had no choice left but to reach out to Him.

> You're blessed when you're at the end of your rope. With less of you there is more of God and his rule (Matthew 5:3 MSG).

The Blessing of Brokenness

As long as you are trying to control your sin on your own—to climb back up your rope—you won't see your need for Jesus. How can you recognize your need for a Savior if you don't even see your need to be saved? Often our desire to be in control—of our sin, our finances, our relationships, or even our life as a whole—is one of the biggest things keeping us from seeing our need for help. For this reason, God knew He would need to remove a lot of distractions from my life before I would be able to see how incapable I was at controlling anything apart from Him.

I believed I could save my marriage if we went through enough counseling, if I read the right books, or if I kept the full truth of my sin hidden from my wife. But then she asked me to move out and I realized I was not in control of my marriage.

I believed I was capable of providing for my family financially. But then I lost my job and I realized I was not in control of my finances.

I believed I could control my sin—including my sexual addiction. But then I met a girl in a bar, made a series of compromises, and ended up in her apartment. I realized I was not in control of my sin.

I realized I wasn't actually in control of anything.

The crap in my life had hit the fan. I had reached a point of brokenness.

I had no choice left but to let go of the end of my rope and give God control of my life.

Three years later, I can honestly tell you it was the best thing I have ever done.

Friends, please understand: *God does not break people.* He does, however, lead us gently to the end of our ropes, where we can finally recognize our brokenness and reach out to Him. This process will probably feel unloving while it is happening, and Satan will try to use that discomfort to convince you that God is not on your side. He will try to deceive you into believing that God is taking good things away from you to hurt you, or that God is cruel and vengeful and wants to punish you for being a failure. None of this is true.

God loves you more than you could ever realize, and it wouldn't be very loving for Him to watch you walk down a road leading to death without trying to stop you at all costs. This is why He sometimes chooses to remove things from our lives—even good things—that are keeping us from recognizing our brokenness. He knows that *temporary* pain is often what it will take for us to reach out to Jesus, who can save us from *eternal* suffering. Sometimes we need to be shaken from our comfort zone and lose our sense of control long enough to see our lives—and our sin—through the lens of His eternal perspective.

You are That Man!

The story of David and Bathsheba from 2 Samuel provides an uncomfortably relevant biblical example of what happens when you attempt to manage your own sin. We often come into this story with David standing on the rooftop and failing to divert his eyes from the bathing beauty, but I think it's important to consider first the attitude of his heart and mind as background.

In the few chapters leading up to this encounter, we see the Lord confirming His blessing over David's life and promising future prosperity for the nation of Israel. We then have an entire chapter recounting all of the armies David defeated and the unbelievable wealth that came to him from the spoils of victory. We are also told of how his fame spread throughout the land, gaining him an almost mythical status. If this were all happening today, he would be on the cover of every magazine. Barbara Walters would interview him. #KingDavid would be trending on Twitter.

David understood that all his success came from God, but the minute he took his focus off of the Lord and attempted to control his own sin, his humble reliance turned into prideful self-confidence. He began to believe, based on his past successes, that he would be capable of managing his life even if he chose to walk independently from God. Unfortunately, David was wrong.

Which brings us back to David on the rooftop. He sees Bathsheba bathing down below and decides to summon her up to his chamber, where the obvious happens. A few weeks later, he receives a note from her with two short, life-changing words: "I'm pregnant."

For David, it's decision time. Does he humble himself before God, admit his sin, and seek God's wisdom in how to proceed; or does he try to cover things up and attempt to control the situation on his own?

David becomes our example of how *not* to respond, unfortunately. He attempts to control the crisis and fix things on his own—apart from God. He invites Bathsheba's husband, Uriah, back from battle and tries to get him to sleep with his wife so everyone will believe the baby is his. When that doesn't work, David gives orders to abandon Uriah in battle so he'll be killed. By orchestrating the murder of Uriah, David can now marry the widowed Bathsheba just in time to make the pregnancy look above board.

Sure, it may have involved deception and murder, but David managed to cover everything up. No one ever needed to find out about his sin. Problem solved, right?

Nope.

David may have believed that he had controlled the sin in his life by managing the outcome, but God knew nothing was actually fixed. In fact, David's attempts at fixing the sin actually made things worse by heaping more sin onto the pile. So God did something very loving for David. He brought him to a point where he could see his own brokenness and recognize his need for God's power in his life once again:

> The Lord sent Nathan the prophet to tell David this story: "There were two men in a certain town. One was rich, and one was poor. The rich man owned a great many sheep and cattle. The poor man owned nothing but one little lamb he had bought. He raised that little lamb, and it grew up with his children. It ate from the man's own plate and drank from his cup. He cuddled it in his arms like a baby daughter. One day a guest arrived at the home of the rich man. But instead of killing an animal from his own flock or herd, he took the poor man's lamb and killed it and prepared it for his guest."
>
> David was furious. "As surely as the LORD lives," he vowed, "any man who would do such a thing deserves to die! He must repay four lambs to the poor man for the one he stole and for having no pity."
>
> Then Nathan said to David, "You are that man!"[2]

In that moment, David came face-to-face with his own brokenness. He realized that he hadn't actually fixed the mess he'd created. He could no longer convince himself that he was in control of his life. He finally saw that this was about more than just saving his reputation or avoiding consequences. He understood that he had sinned against the Lord.[3]

He stopped pretending that everything in his life was okay and chose to own his sin—all of it. He owned the way it kept his eyes off God. He owned the pain it caused in the lives of others. He stopped justifying, hiding, and making excuses for it. He finally chose to accept full responsibility for his actions—including the painful consequences he knew would follow as a result.

Some time later, after this encounter with Nathan, David wrote Psalm 51, where he paints a haunting picture of how attempting to handle his own sin robbed him of all joy or peace. This psalm also gives us a beautiful

2 2 Samuel 12:1–7.

3 2 Samuel 12:13.

example of how sin actually can be dealt with once we take responsibility for it and recognize our brokenness:

> You do not desire a sacrifice, or I would offer one.
> You do not want a burnt offering.
> The sacrifice you desire is a broken spirit.
> You will not reject a broken and repentant heart, O God (Psalm 51:16–17).

David understood there was no way he could make amends for his sin. There was nothing he could do to make things right. He knew the way back to close intimacy with God wasn't to try and fix things, control his sin, or earn God's favor. It was to recognize his brokenness, own his sin, and run back to the Lord with a spirit of repentance.

Repentance—The Only Way to Deal with Your Sin

If you've grown up in the church, you've undoubtedly heard a lot about repentance. We commonly define repentance as "turning away from your sin and turning back to God." This is true, of course, but it's also easy to misunderstand what biblical repentance looks like, even within this definition.

For many years, I believed I had a correct understanding of biblical repentance, but it turns out my definition was off in a few critical ways. I was looking at repentance as something I could offer to God rather than a gift that God was offering to me. I was viewing it as a promise to have better behavior rather than a desperate cry for help to overcome my bad behavior. Based on that, my definition of repentance was much closer to this:

> [Promising to] turn away from my sin [by working harder on it] and running back to God [after I reached a point of making myself acceptable again].

What I thought was an act of repentance was actually just the opposite. In fact, my sin laughed at my attempts to work on it. That's because true repentance involves placing your sin under the power of the cross—the only power strong enough to destroy it. It may seem contradictory, but choosing to give up the fight against your sin is the only attack against it that will bring lasting results.

Ultimately, repentance is choosing to believe that God's grace is true—even for you. It's looking at your sin and realizing God has provided a way of escape that you could never have created on your own.[4] It's placing yourself—and your sin—under His mercy, and realizing He wants to destroy the sin in your life instead of destroying you.

In light of that, a better definition of repentance would be this:

> Turning away from your sin [because you recognize you can't handle it on your own], and turning back to God [the only one who has to power to overcome it].

There you go. Now you know the answer to sin. You can stop reading and go on to live a perfect, sinless life from here on out. There's just one problem with that, however. We're all still human, which means we're all still going to sin on occasion. Lucky for us, God knows this and loves us regardless. So the real question isn't "How do I live a sinless life?" but "How do I respond when I do sin?"

The answer, of course, is to recognize your brokenness, respond with repentance, and run back to Jesus. But there's a sneaky substitute you need to be aware of that can deceive us into believing we are repentant when, in fact, we are still continuing to walk independently from God.

Remorse vs. Repentance

There are two men in the Bible whose lives help illustrate what these two different responses to our sin look like, as well as the result that comes from following each path to the end. Both of these men were close disciples of Jesus who had sinned against Him, quickly recognized their sin, and chose to turn away from it. One responded by attempting to fix his sin on his own—remorse. The other responded by running back to Jesus—repentance.

4 1 Corinthians 10:13.

The Unfortunate Result of Remorse

For three years, Judas went everywhere with Jesus. He saw every miracle. He heard every sermon. He talked with Jesus and lived with Him. They sat around campfires, shared meals, and were more than likely very close friends. Even with all that time together, Judas never gave his heart fully to his rabbi. He couldn't let go of his sense of control.

Judas was the treasurer for the disciples and managed their communal finances, so we can assume he was trusted. But we also know he had a pattern of stealing some of the money for himself.[5] In order to maintain his ruse of being trustworthy, he would have had to become an expert at deception and dishonesty. We see this deception at work when he argues that the woman who was anointing Jesus with expensive perfume was being financially irresponsible.[6] He wasn't being sacrificial and generous by suggesting she should have sold the perfume and given the money to the poor—he was attempting to make himself *appear* sacrificial and generous to cover up his own selfish love of money.

Judas was more interested in controlling his *external* appearance than finding a solution for his *internal* sinfulness. He may have felt bad about his sin, but it was only because he was afraid getting exposed would harm his reputation. He felt the need to hide his sin, but he didn't hate it yet. He hadn't come to a point of brokenness where he saw the full effect of his sinfulness and desired to turn from it no matter the cost.

This was the same way I approached my pornography addiction for years. I always felt bad about it, but if I had been honest it wasn't because I hated the sin itself. I felt bad about looking at porn because I knew getting caught would cost me a lot. My remorse was based on my own selfishness. The problem with this way of thinking, though, is it actually caused my sin to increase.

When you try to control your sin on your own, especially when your motivation to change is self-centered, there are three things that typically happen as a result:

---

5 John 12:6.

6 John 12:4–5.

1. Your attempt at controlling your sin (and inability to do so) will cause you to become more aware of it, which will lead you to view yourself as a failure.

2. You will then justify, make allowances, or create excuses for your sin as an attempt to minimize these growing negative feelings about yourself.

3. These compromises will cause your heart to gradually become calloused. Eventually, you will no longer feel the same level of guilt and may even reach a point of no longer feeling bad about your sin at all.

If you've ever learned to play the guitar, you have experienced what it means to become calloused. At first, your fingers are tender and it's uncomfortable to press down on the strings. Over time, though, if you continue to repeat the action of pressing your fingers against the strings, you will develop hard calluses on the pressure areas. Once these calluses are present, you no longer feel the pressure anymore.

The same process happens with your heart when you repeatedly justify or make excuses for your sin. Each time you do this, your heart becomes a tiny bit more calloused. The guilt you used to feel as a result of your sin gets quieter and quieter. Eventually, justifying it becomes so natural you reach a point where you no longer feel guilt at all.

> When a man is getting better, he understands more and more clearly the evil that's left in him. When a man is getting worse, he understands his own badness less and less.[7]

This is the reason very few men start off by looking at extremely explicit pornography. They usually begin with soft-core porn before progressing to the more hard-core. If you were to show pictures from a fetish site to a man who was just getting into porn, he would probably be shocked and

7 C.S. Lewis, *Mere Christianity* (New York: HarperCollins, 2001).

appalled. Within a few years, though, if his sin is left unchecked, he might come to find those same images to be tame.

The excuses and allowances you make to justify your sin will slowly drag you in deeper and deeper over time. And because it happens so subtly, you rarely notice until it's too late. My own addiction progressed from lingerie ads in the Sunday paper, to topless porn, to full nudity, to hard-core, to videos, to chat rooms, and eventually to full-on adultery. My teenage self would have found the adult version of me to be a shockingly immoral pervert. In reality, I was still the same man. The only difference was, my heart had become hardened and calloused through years of unrepentant sin.

In the same way, Judas' continual justification and excuse-making led to the hardening of his heart. What began with taking a few coins out of the disciples' money bag for his own pocket grew to the point of selling Jesus to the temple guards for 30 pieces of silver. When Judas later found out His rabbi had been condemned to die, he was horrified.

I believe this was the point where Judas finally came face-to-face with his own brokenness. The Bible tells us that "he was filled with *remorse*" (not repentance). So he took the thirty pieces of silver back to the leading priests and the elders to try and undo what he had done."[8] Just like David, he tried to manage the fallout and fix his sin on his own.

When the priests and elders laughed off his attempt to pay them back, Judas realized he couldn't undo it this time and became full of despair. Fearing what a life lived under a cloud of unending guilt and remorse would be like, he chose to take his own life, and he hung himself.

The Freedom of Repentance

Peter, on the other hand, didn't even need a sack of money to walk away from Jesus. All it took for him was a teenage girl asking whether he was associated with the man who was on trial for treason.

The day before His trial, Jesus told Peter he would deny Him three times before the rooster crowed. Peter, as usual, was overconfident and vowed to stay with Jesus no matter what—even to the point of death. But

8 Matthew 27:3.

Jesus knew His disciple would get caught up in his own self-protection and deny him nonetheless. Sure enough, Peter denied Jesus repeatedly that night. Immediately after his third denial, he looked up and caught the eyes of Jesus...as the sound of the rooster's crow pierced his heart. The memory of Jesus' words came flooding back into his mind as he realized what he had just done. He began to weep, and ran out of the courtyard full of despair. Peter had recognized his own brokenness.

Judas and Peter both turned their backs on their Lord in similar ways. Judas went on to take his own life, but Peter ended up giving his entire life to Jesus. Why did their lives turn out so differently? It's because the path of your life is impacted more by your response to your sin than the act of sinning itself. The reason Peter's life turned out better was because he chose the biblical response to his sin. He ran back to Jesus in repentance.

The second that Peter heard the rumors of Jesus' resurrection, he ran to the tomb to see for himself if it was true. He couldn't wait to see Jesus again because He desperately wanted to be restored to Him. Peter hated the sin he had committed—not because of what it had cost him, but because it had broken the heart of Jesus. He also knew his sin was a product of his own brokenness, and only Jesus had the power to put him back together and make him whole again. He recognized how badly he needed Him.

When Peter arrived at the tomb, it was empty. Jesus was nowhere to be found. This was great, of course, because it gave him hope that Jesus really was alive. But he was also confused and didn't know what was going on. Was Jesus alive, or had someone stolen the body?

A week or so later, Peter and a few other disciples were out fishing when a man showed up and started cooking on the shore. He yelled out, asking the guys if they had caught anything. They hadn't. So the man proceeded to tell them to throw the net over the other side of the boat—the same thing Jesus had told them when He first met them. Immediately their eyes were opened and they recognized the man. It was Jesus!

> Then the disciple Jesus loved said to Peter, "It's the Lord!" When Simon Peter heard that it was the Lord, he put on his tunic (for he had stripped for work), jumped into the water, and

> headed to shore. The others stayed with the boat and pulled the loaded net to the shore, for they were only about a hundred yards from shore. When they got there, they found breakfast waiting for them—fish cooking over a charcoal fire, and some bread (John 21:7–9).

When Peter saw Jesus, he didn't even wait for everyone to row the boat to shore. He jumped into the lake, clothes and all, and swam as fast as he could to get back to Jesus.

Now, think about this. If Peter had been planning to come up with a point-by-point explanation justifying why he denied Jesus and a list of the changes he had made to show Him how he had his sin under control now, wouldn't He have rowed *slowly* to shore to give himself time to think through the best way to present his argument? If you're scheduled for a trial to defend yourself of something you know you are guilty of and you see the judge walking down the street, are you going to run to him like a Labrador chasing a squirrel? Of course not.

So it seems clear that Peter wasn't swimming to Jesus in order to try and make things right on his own. He was swimming to Him because he realized nothing else mattered apart from being restored to Him. No matter what it cost him, Peter *had* to be back with Jesus.

That, my friends, is repentance!

There's no doubt that Peter felt far away from Jesus. He felt as if his sin had driven a wedge between him and his Lord. Many believers today would say that Peter had "fallen out of fellowship" with Jesus because of his sin. Some even feel like God turns His back on them when they fall into temptation. But if that were the case, how do you reconcile it with Romans 8?

> I am convinced that neither death nor life, neither angels nor demons, neither the present nor the future, nor any powers, neither height nor depth, nor anything else in all creation, will be able to separate us from the love of God that is in Christ Jesus our Lord (Romans 8:38–39).

Why did Peter feel the need to be restored if nothing was able to separate him from the love of God?

Well, what if Peter never was separated?

Friends, once you are in Christ, your sin will never separate you from God. Never. If, however, you try to control or justify your sin, it means you have taken your focus off God and put it back on your sin. When you focus on what defined who you were in your old way of living (before Christ) rather than what defines who you are now (in Christ), you will *feel* as if you are once again living apart from Christ. Your *focus* will greatly affect your *feelings*.

A husband may live in the same house and even sleep in the same bed with his wife, but still feel very much alone. If he never talks to her, constantly hides things from her, and is merely going through the motions of relationship while his heart and mind are elsewhere, he will need to repent before intimacy will ever return. In this case, repentance is turning from his sins of neglect and fantasy and turning back to engage his wife. Even if his wife never leaves him and remains present, he will continue to feel isolated from her until he places his focus back on her.

But here's the cool thing about all of this—Jesus came to find Peter. And not just Peter, but all the disciples. Every one of these guys needed to come back to their Lord after they had abandoned him during his trial. But Jesus didn't wait for them to come to Him. He hunted them down. And it wasn't to make them grovel and beg for His forgiveness. He showed up to cook His friends breakfast and hang out with them around the campfire again.

Jesus knew Peter *felt* separated, however, which is why He took the opportunity to remind him how much he was loved. He affirmed Peter three times—once for each time His disciple had denied Him. He reminded Peter of his new identity, which gave him the strength to walk in a manner worthy of the calling God had placed on his life. He told Peter, "I'm still with you. I believe in you. Now go and do what I've called you to do."

In the same way, Jesus is actively seeking restoration with you as well. You may feel as if you have ran far away from Him, but in reality, He never even let you get away in the first place. If you turn around, you'll find Him standing right there with you—arms wide open, waiting to welcome you back.

How Does This Help Me with Porn?

You may have decided you are sick of pornography and vowed to turn away from it for good. But as long as you are still trying to fight it, you will continue to think about it. And what happens when you think about fighting porn? You think even more about the very images you are trying to resist thinking about. The act of trying to fight pornography actually causes you to dwell on it even more.

It's the same thing that happens if I ask you not to think about a pink elephant...

You're thinking about a pink elephant, aren't you? Yeah, me too.

As ridiculous as that illustration may be, it illustrates how focusing on fighting your sin actually causes you to sin more. Your mind will always move toward whatever it is thinking about, even if you are thinking about what you want to avoid. Which is why Jesus never asks you to focus on fixing your sin, He asks you to focus on Him—the only One who can lead you to freedom from your sin.

If you focus on Jesus and how He has set you free, you will automatically draw closer to Him, which will result in you becoming more like Him. And the more you become like Jesus, the less you will sin. This process of becoming more like Him is commonly called *sanctification*. It's the same process Paul is talking about here in his letter to the Philippians:

> Brothers and sisters, I do not consider myself yet to have taken hold of it. But one thing I do: Forgetting what is behind and straining toward what is ahead, I press on toward the goal to win the prize for which God has called me heavenward in Christ Jesus (Philippians 3:13–14).

Paul's response wasn't to strive toward sanctifying himself by working on his sin. Not at all. He chose to forget what was behind (his sin), and strain toward what was ahead (Jesus). He recognized that sanctification is a process that begins on earth and will only reach completion in heaven. He also knew that sanctification could only be done by the work of Jesus, not the work of Paul. So instead of focusing on the process (which he wasn't even in control of), he chose to focus on the end goal (life with Jesus). Paul understood that we naturally move toward whatever we focus on, so he chose to stop dwelling on his sin and to focus only on Jesus.

The more you come to see God for who He really is—a loving Father, full of grace and mercy, who wants only what's best for you—the more likely you will be to trust His offer of repentance. You will no longer fear the consequences of owning your sin, because you know God will walk through it with you. If, however, you still see Him as an angry judge who is looking for opportunities to "correct" your behavior with lightning bolts and punishment, you won't want to ask for His help. It will feel safer to keep fighting on your own and hiding from His perceived judgment. This is why viewing repentance as a gift of grace helps you to trust that God isn't asking you to turn from your sin because He wants to kill all of your fun. He's asking you to turn from your sin because He knows the damage and pain it will cause in your life.

Peter may have had to wait until he saw the resurrected Jesus in person to repent and be restored, but now that Jesus has ascended back to heaven and the Holy Spirit lives inside of us, we can run back to Jesus at any time. We don't need to wait, because we are never more than a prayer away from His help in our time of need.

When the temptation to look at pornography does come, don't focus on resisting it. Focus on trusting Jesus. Pray to Him and ask for His strength to walk away. Dwell on the truth of Scripture and remind yourself who you are now that you are in Christ. Remember, striving to resist porn will never set you free. Only the truth of Scripture will set you free.

When you do give in to sin—we all will at times—don't be afraid to run back to Jesus right away. Trust that the grace of God covers you, which means you are still loved and accepted fully. Don't wait until you feel like you are strong enough or good enough to come back to Jesus, because the whole point of repentance is recognizing that you never will reach that point.

God doesn't want you to keep trying to be holy. He wants you to actually *be* holy.[9] But the only way to truly be holy is to deal with your sin according to His terms and not your own. And His path to holiness—to

---

9 1 Peter 1:16.

sanctification—is repentance. The response He desires from you isn't to try and control your sin, but to believe the truth of John 15:5:

> I am the vine; you are the branches. If you remain in me and I in you, you will bear much fruit; *apart from me you can do nothing* (John 15:5).

Don't just turn away from your sin. Turn back to Jesus, for apart from Him, you can do nothing.

LIE #7

Jesus Can Set Others Free from Pornography Addiction, but Not Me

This is your last chance. After this, there is no turning back...You take the red pill—you stay in Wonderland and I show you how deep the rabbit-hole goes.

MORPHEUS, *THE MATRIX*

I don't mean to brag or anything, but I live in the most beautiful state in the Union. Sure, some states have great beaches. Some states have great mountains. You can find amazing forests in Vermont and spectacular deserts in Arizona. Oregon, however, has all of these. So, as you frequently hear on ESPN during football season...Oregon wins.

A few months back I went for a hike to Steelhead Falls, a 25-foot waterfall along the Deschutes River in the high desert of Central Oregon. I had only been planning on a leisurely hike, but once I reached the falls, plans changed. I ran into a group of college kids jumping off the cliffs into the river below. Immediately, the part of my brain that still thinks I'm a teenager began pushing me to jump off the cliff as well.

Come on, old man! It's hot. The water is perfect. Everyone else is jumping in, so you know it's safe. Do it! What's the matter, McFly? You chicken?

I took off my backpack, stripped down to my shorts, walked to the edge of the cliff, looked down at the water...

Nope.

Fear showed up. Logic kicked in. I came up with many compelling and well-thought-out excuses of why this was a terrible idea.

I backed away from the cliff.

We do the exact same thing with God, don't we?

When was the last time you felt Him leading you to do something that made no sense or was outside of your comfort zone? Perhaps it was an urge to share your faith with a friend. Maybe you felt you needed to ask forgiveness from someone you had wronged. For me, it was coming clean and confessing the full extent of my pornography addiction and adultery to my wife.

Why would I ever do that? That makes no sense at all.

But God's ways aren't always logical in the eyes of man. He knew the only way I could ever be free from my addiction, and the only way our marriage could ever heal, was if I brought everything into the light where it could finally be dealt with.

I wrestled with God for years on coming clean. I kept inching up to the cliff, looking over the edge, and saying no. I was too afraid it would cost me my marriage. I kept telling God He didn't know what He was asking me to do. I convinced myself that what He was asking simply wasn't logical.

I wasn't being logical, though. I was being a coward.

I looked for other ways down to the water, such as marriage books or counseling, but those roads never led anywhere. I tried wading into the water slowly by confessing only part of my sin to her, but that only caused pain without opening the door for any real healing.

Ultimately, I didn't believe God could be trusted.

But He kept standing right there with me, gently saying, "Jump, my son. Jump into this adventure of faith. There is no other way to get to where I want to take you. Just trust me in this. It's worth it."

And so one day, when I realized I had no other options left, I jumped. I confessed everything to my wife. Yes, there were tears. There was immense pain. The consequences were devastating.

But in that moment—when I finally jumped in and trusted God no matter how illogical it seemed—He became real to me.

You can believe jumping off the cliff is safe. You can watch others do it. You can admire the drop from the top, carefully climb down the rocks, and dip a toe in the water. But no matter what you do, if you don't jump off the cliff, you will never experience the thrill of jumping off the cliff. There's just no way to experience it halfway.

Likewise, you can't go halfway with Jesus. If you aren't all in, you're not really in at all. You must come to a point where you trust Him enough to jump off that cliff.

Being all in is not about being perfect. It's about believing that Jesus really is the Son of God, that He knows what's best for you, and trusting whatever He asks you to do *no matter what*. It's an absolute trust that *every* word, *every* promise, and *every* blessing spoken in the Bible is true—even for you—whether it feels true or not.

TRUTH: If you believe Jesus is Lord, you can trust that everything He promises is true, even for you.

The Difference Between Belief and Faith

We often think the key to following Jesus is simply to believe in Him. But if belief were all that mattered, even the demons would be saved.[1] The demons may *believe* in God, but they don't *trust* Him. They don't have faith—an absolute trust that everything the Word of God says is true.

A well-known story tells of a tightrope walker entertaining a crowd at Niagara Falls. At first, he simply walked across a cable strung above the waterfall, but as the crowd grew, he continued to up the stakes. He did a lap while juggling and another lap blindfolded. He even rode a bike across the line. The crowd watched in amazement, wondering what he would attempt next.

As he returned to the side of the river where many had gathered to watch, he got off his bike and pulled out a wheelbarrow. He then turned to address the crowd.

"Do you believe I can walk across this tightrope without falling?"

1 James 2:19.

"Yes!" roared the crowd.

"Do you believe I can walk across this tightrope while pushing this wheelbarrow?"

"We do!" they yelled.

"Do you believe I can walk across this tightrope while pushing this wheelbarrow with someone riding in it?"

The crowd went nuts. They couldn't wait to see this trick.

"Then who would like to volunteer to be my rider?"

Silence.

Every person in the crowd may have believed he could do it, but no one was willing to trust him by getting into the wheelbarrow. So in reality, even though they said they believed he could do it, their lack of trust proved they didn't.

This distinction is important to understand: What you *say* you believe is not necessarily what you do believe. Even what you *think* you believe may not be what you truly believe. What you *do* and what you *trust* are what exposes your true beliefs. In this way, faith is belief that is backed by trust and therefore results in action.

Everybody has faith in something. For many, it's faith in their own wisdom or abilities. For others, it's faith in a religion or in rituals. But if your true faith isn't in Jesus, it will never result in a changed life. That's because faith is only as strong as its object, and the only "object" that has the power to change you is Jesus.

We see this misplaced faith in the Pharisees all throughout the Gospels. These men trusted in their knowledge of the Scriptures and their ability to follow the Law to give them life. They studied the Scriptures diligently, but when they met Jesus, they refused to take the next step by putting their faith in Him:

> You have your heads in your Bibles constantly because you think you'll find eternal life there. But you miss the forest for the trees. These Scriptures are all about me! And here I am, standing right before you, and you aren't willing to receive from me the life you say you want (John 5:39–40 MSG),

These men believed the Scriptures, but when Jesus asked them to trust in Him to find the life they were looking for, they chose not to get in the wheelbarrow.

Just like these Pharisees, if you believe in Jesus but don't trust Him enough to do what He's asking you to do, you will keep looking for other things to make you feel like you are actually following Him. But you will miss out on the blessings of knowing Christ. Not because His blessings are not true, but because you are looking for ways to receive them without actually trusting Him. Many people interpret this lack of blessing as a sign that Jesus isn't working for them. In reality, it's a sign that they aren't trusting in Him—they are still trusting in themselves.

Don't interpret this as a call to buck up and try harder. You may be thinking, *I just need to work up some more faith! I need to follow God's rules better!* These may sound like the righteous things to do, but by doing them you would be putting your faith back on yourself and your own ability to please God. None of us will ever be able to generate more faith on our own, though, because—like repentance—faith is a gift that God gives to you.

So if you feel the need for more faith, don't try to muster it up on your own. Pray like the man who approached Jesus, asking Him to free his son from demonic oppression:

> "I do believe, but help me overcome my unbelief!" (Mark 9:24).

Trust + Action = Faith that Changes Lives

When God calls you to do something that requires tremendous trust—to "take a leap of faith" as we sometimes say—He isn't doing it to *test your ability to generate* faith. He is doing it to *offer you an opportunity to receive* more faith. The more you trust Him, the more He allows your faith to grow.

This makes sense when you think about it. God has perfect knowledge, power over everything, and wants only what is best for you—so you can be confident He will never let you down or lose control of any situation. He will never fail you or leave you hanging. Every time you trust Him, He will come through for you. It may not be in the way you were expecting or hoping for, but it will always be for your best. When you experience His trustworthiness in your life over and over, it becomes easier to trust Him when He calls you to exercise faith in the future—not because of your ability to trust, but because of His unblemished track record.

But if you don't trust God's unconditional love for you, you will never be confident that He really is acting in your best interest. You will always be questioning His trustworthiness based on whether you feel you have been good enough to earn it or not. You will weigh everything He calls you to do on an imaginary continuum: *Is God calling me to do this to better me, or to punish me?* You will only trust Him to the degree that you understand how much He loves you, which is why having a proper understanding of His grace is key for life-changing faith to even be a possibility.

You can be certain, however, that God does love you—no matter how messed up you may feel—and everything He calls you to do is for your benefit. The more you trust in this truth, the more your faith will grow. Eventually, you will come to realize that you really can trust *everything* Jesus promises to be true—even for you—no matter how illogical or unbelievable it may seem. The blessings of the faith you read about in the Bible will become increasingly real to you, not because you have suddenly earned them or deserve them more, but because you are finally trusting them to be true.

Let's look at a few of these blessings and see how trusting Jesus determines whether we experience them in our lives or not.

Trusting Jesus Leads to Rest

When you are burnt out and exhausted, there is nothing that feels better than rest. It's the only thing that can recharge you. Jesus understood this deep desire for rest within us, which is why He frequently combined His offer of life with the promise of rest:

> Jesus said, "Come to me, all of you who are weary and carry heavy burdens, and I will give you rest" (Matthew 11:28).

> "Take my yoke upon you. Let me teach you, because I am humble and gentle at heart, and you will find rest for your souls" (Matthew 11:29).

Jesus clearly promised rest for all who follow Him, so why are so many of us burning out? Why are we exhausting ourselves trying to live moral lives but still going nowhere?

To answer that question, let's take a look at Hebrews 4:1–2:

> God's promise of entering his rest still stands, so we ought to tremble with fear that some of you might fail to experience it. For this good news—that God has prepared this rest—has been announced to us just as it was to them. *But it did them no good because they didn't share the faith of those who listened to God* (Hebrews 4:1–2).

The writer of Hebrews makes it clear that God's offer of rest is still good. The reason some who were professing faith in Christ hadn't experienced it was because they didn't actually trust what Jesus had done for them. They said they had faith in Him, but their actions proved otherwise. They weren't experiencing rest because they wouldn't stop working on their own salvation.

A few verses later, we see how fully believing in Jesus really does lead to rest:

> All who have entered into God's rest have rested from their labors, just as God did after creating the world (Hebrews 4:10).

In order to experience God's rest, you must trust Jesus when He says there is no work left to do in regard to your salvation. You must believe that it really is finished. Hang up your hat, sit down with Jesus, and rest in the fact that He has already completed the work for you.

To further clarify this, let's look at a few behaviors that may expose a belief that there is still work left for you to do:

- Do you keep asking for forgiveness every time you sin? Could that be a sign that you don't believe Jesus when He says all your sins were forgiven at the time of His death?[2] If you don't believe

2 Ephesians 1:7.

your sins are already forgiven, you will keep trying to earn more forgiveness.

- Are you going to confession to seek restoration from a priest? What does that say about your trust that Jesus is the only mediator between God and man,[3] or your ability to have access to the throne of God?[4] If you don't believe you can speak directly with Jesus, you will seek out religious rituals in order to feel spiritual.

- Do you keep making promises to God to become a better person? Is that a sign that you don't really believe you have already been transformed into a new creation?[5] If you don't believe you have been changed, you will keep trying to change yourself.

All of these actions expose a belief that Jesus needs your help to save you. There is still work to be done. But no matter how hard you try to contribute, these things will never work. And as long as you keep chasing after them, you will never be able to rest.

The only thing that will provide rest is to trust that every word Jesus said was true—even for you. Trust that your salvation is secure and rest in the fact that the work is done.

> Only we who believe can enter his rest (Hebrews 4:3).

Trusting Jesus Leads to Peace

The harder things get in life, the more we need to trust in the faithfulness of Jesus. If you choose to trust Him—even in the midst of trials—you will see Him come through every time. This is how trials can actually breed trust. They give you an opportunity to experience God's rescuing you.

The verse I have had to remind myself to trust time and time again when life gets hard is Romans 8:28:

---

3 1 Timothy 2:5.

4 Hebrews 4:16.

5 2 Corinthians 5:17.

> We know that God causes everything to work together for the good of those who love God and are called according to his purpose for them (Romans 8:28).

This verse doesn't say that all things are good, or that God will make all things good. It also doesn't say He will never allow anything bad to happen. What it does say is that He will cause all things—even the bad things—to produce good results in the lives of those who have trusted in Him.

But do you honestly believe that? When something blows up in your life, do you trust that He is using it for your ultimate good? Again, what does your behavior expose about your true belief?

Imagine you just got caught looking at porn on your computer at work and got fired. What is your response? Chances are, your first response will be fear and worry. What will you tell your wife? What if everybody finds out why you were fired? How will you pay the bills? Will you ever find another job?

It may be natural to respond this way, but it will not lead you to peace.

But what if you choose to believe that God is able to use all things for your good, even a terrible situation such as this? By looking for ways He is using the situation for your good, you might see it as Him deciding it's time for your sin to come into the light where it can be dealt with. That would actually be a good thing—I personally know of half a dozen men who got caught looking at porn at work, and this became the first step on their journey to freedom. Maybe God knew you needed to find a new job because He had something better for you and knew you would never leave on your own. (This was ultimately why He allowed me to lose my job.) Perhaps He knew your flirtations with the secretary were likely to grow into something more sinister and chose to remove you from the temptation. It could be many different things.

The truth is, even if you don't trust this verse, God would still be working behind the scenes in this difficult situation to use it for your good. Not trusting Him and choosing to worry—or worse yet, struggling to control the situation—wouldn't necessarily change the outcome, but it would rob you of His peace. Which is why trusting that He really is working in your best interest is key to experiencing His peace in your life.

In my own life, there are many areas where I need to trust God's leading instead of following whatever feels right to me at that moment. The biggest example is probably the decision to remain committed to—and wait for—my former wife.

God has made it clear to me through a variety of ways that He wants me to leave the door open for the possibility of reconciliation. All throughout Scripture I see Him restoring and re-creating what is broken rather than creating something altogether new. I hear the command to love my wife as Christ loved the church, and He has continued to love the church even as they have rejected Him over and over. Ultimately, God has put His unconditional love in my heart for her—which means my love for her is not conditional on her returning any love to me.

If I am being honest, though, there are many days I am tempted to listen to my friends when they tell me it's time to move on. Sometimes, when I find myself becoming interested in a girl, my mind starts to wander into what-if situations. I begin to justify in my mind reasons why it would make more sense for me to start dating again. After all, what happens if my wife remains single for ten years and then marries someone else? At that point, I'll be older and balder and won't be able to find a spouse even if I wanted to.

But God never promised that my wife and I would get back together—He only asked me to wait for her. For all I know, the good in my life He is orchestrating through this time of waiting may be something completely different than the restoration of our marriage.

Perhaps He knew I would not have had the time to write this book if I had been dating. Maybe His purpose is for my singleness to be an example to other men of how much pornography can cost them. Maybe He knows I wouldn't have been able to serve Him as well if I'd been in a relationship right now. I just don't know.

What I do know is, even if He doesn't bring us back together, He's doing something good through my waiting. So I'll keep pursuing my former wife as long as Jesus keeps pursuing me (which is always). And trusting Him in this area allows me to respond with thankfulness rather than worrying about my life.

> Don't worry about anything; instead, pray about everything. Tell God what you need, and thank him for all he has done. Then you will experience God's peace, which exceeds anything we can understand (Philippians 4:6–7).

Instead of worrying about whether or not I'll be single for the rest of my life, I can leave it all in God's hands, remember the ways He has taken care of me, and trust He will continue to lead me down the best path for my life.

And trusting Him for that gives me peace.

Trusting Jesus Leads to Dependency

Doesn't it sound strange to say that it's a good thing to be dependent? Obviously, that assertion depends on the object of your dependence. Being dependent on alcohol is a big problem, but being dependent on Christ frees you from trying to maintain control, which will keep you from experiencing God's rest and peace.

In order to fully trust God, though, you need to trust that He knows how to run your life better than you do. But more than that, you must submit to His leading and depend on Him for guidance. If you're still trying to be the one in the driver's seat, only seeing God as your co-pilot, it shows you don't really believe He can lead you. You are still trusting in your own ability to drive.

Once again, author Bob George has the perfect illustration to help us understand this concept:

> Picture yourself in one of those old drivers-education cars. If you remember, these cars had two steering wheels, two gas pedals, two brakes, and so forth. Pretend you're in one seat, and the Lord is in the other. He says to you, "My child, I have great plans for you. I will reveal Myself to you, shower you with My love and acceptance, set you free by renewing your mind with My truth, and conform you to My image as we go through life together. All you have to do is enjoy the ride and let Me

> drive. But notice that in front of you is your own set of driving controls. You have the capability and freedom of grabbing the steering wheel and taking things into your own hands. Only one of us can drive at a time, and the choice is yours. If you take control, I will take My hands off. I promise that, whatever you choose, I will never leave you or forsake you. But isn't it far better to allow Me to drive? I love you. I have all wisdom, all power, and I am committed to your ultimate good. I ask you to trust Me, but you are always free to choose."[6]

You will always have the ability to seize control and call the shots in your own life. But if you trust that God knows everything—including the future—and is guiding you in a way that will lead you to what is best for you, why would you ever want to take over? If you knew everything He knew, wouldn't you choose to do the exact same things He is asking you to do?

This can be really hard to wrap your brain around, especially when it comes to our sin. Because sometimes, even if you are trusting in Christ alone to set you free from your sin, you still sin. Why would God, who has all the power to make it so you never sin again, allow you the freedom to still sin on occasion? How can that be what's best for you?

Look at what Paul had to say about a similar struggle in his life:

> I was given a thorn in my flesh, a messenger from Satan to torment me and keep me from becoming proud. Three different times I begged the Lord to take it away. Each time he said, "My grace is all you need. My power works best in weakness." So now I am glad to boast about my weaknesses, so that the power of Christ can work through me. That's why I take pleasure in my weaknesses, and in the insults, hardships, persecutions, and troubles that I suffer for Christ. For when I am weak, then I am strong (2 Corinthians 12:7–10).

We don't know for sure what the thorn in Paul's flesh really was. Some

6 Bob George, *Faith That Pleases God* (Eugene, OR: Harvest House Publishers, 2001), 33.

people think it was a painful physical illness. Some say it was his continual struggle with a particular sin, like what we see him talking about at the end of Romans 7. What we do know for sure is that its source was demonic, yet God still used it for Paul's good.

Paul pleaded multiple times for God to take this thorn away. But for some reason, God kept saying no. God knew that if He healed His servant from this particular struggle, he would become proud. With the thorn remaining, Paul had a constant reminder of his need for God's power to overcome his weaknesses. It kept him from ever thinking he had "arrived" or becoming self-sufficient. By trusting that God was working for His good even if He didn't answer his prayer in the way he was hoping for, Paul was able to recognize God's grace and power at work in his life and respond with thankfulness.

I'm going to tell you something that may surprise you, being that I'm writing a book on overcoming pornography addiction. About once or twice a year, I still lose the battle. It's my thorn in the flesh. I've asked God to free me from this completely, and His answer is still "Not yet."

And I'm okay with that.

I know myself well enough to know that if I never sinned again, I would quickly forget what the struggle was like. I would become boastful and full of pride. I would lose any compassion or understanding for the men I'm trying to help and would dish out arrogant lectures about how they just need to try harder to be perfect like me.

That guy scares me.

Now, I'm not saying it's okay to sin. I hate the fact that I don't have this 100 percent nailed yet. I know God has promised to complete His work in me, but I also understand it won't be finished until the day that Christ returns.[7] Which means even though I'm getting better, I will never be perfect. At least not until I get to heaven. Even if God does bring me to a point where I never lose another battle with porn again, I'll just struggle with something else.

So for now, I'll trust that He has me on His schedule for sanctification,

---

7 Philippians 1:6.

not mine. Maybe next time I'll go a full year, and then two, and then five… But for reasons only He fully knows, He thinks once or twice a year is the best spot for me at this point.

A Little Clarification…

Some of you are completely freaking out right now about what you just read. I get that. I was in the same camp for many years. But understand me here. I'm not justifying my sin. There is nothing I would like more than to be rid of this completely. But if the apostle Paul, who is undoubtedly near the top of the Bible Hall of Fame, couldn't reach a point of sinless perfection in this life, how can we ever expect to? Paul trusted God's grace to cover his lack of perfection, so we can as well.

If perfection isn't a possibility for you (and if you're being honest with yourself, you know it's the truth), then what do you do with your inevitable slip-ups? You can hide them, but that will lead to isolation. You can justify them, but that will harden your heart. You can try harder to overcome them, but that will keep you focused on fulfilling the law rather than trusting grace. Any of those roads will cause you to miss Jesus.

Think it over. Does God's grace really cover the sin that still surfaces in your life? And there is nothing wrong with asking Him to show you why He is allowing your thorn to remain. I trust that He will give you an answer, but it's up to you whether you trust it or not.

Trusting Jesus Leads to Relationship

I can't tell you how many times I've heard the saying "It's not about religion, it's about relationship." I've even used it myself at times. In a lot of ways, it's the foundational truth that this entire book is based on. But have you actually stopped to consider what that saying is trying to communicate? It's the idea that following Jesus is not about living up to some moral standard or performing certain rituals—it's about actually getting to know Him and spending time with Him. It's about having a *relationship* with Him.

But what does a personal relationship with Jesus actually look like? For that matter, what does a relationship with anyone look like?

In order for any relationship to develop, you must spend time with each other. You must seek to know each other on a personal level. Most importantly, you must trust one another. If you remove any one of these elements from the relationship, it will never grow into a meaningful friendship.

It's the same with a relationship with Jesus. You can spend time with Him in prayer. You can seek to know all about Him by reading the Bible. But if you don't trust Him, you will never experience a true relationship with Him.

The moment I came clean about the full depth of my sin—I've mentioned this a few times already—was the moment Jesus became real to me. Before that moment, if I was being honest, I called myself a follower of Jesus. But I didn't know Him personally. I didn't have a relationship with Him.

Sure, I knew all *about* Jesus. I had grown up in church and had even gone to seminary, so I knew all the answers to the Bible trivia questions. I even spent time with Him—sort of. I prayed to Him on a regular basis, but it was only when I needed something, never because I just wanted to hang out with Him. As soon as He asked me to do anything that pushed me or required me to trust Him, I would find an excuse to ignore Him. I was fine trusting Him with *most* things, but I didn't want to trust Him with *everything*. I still wouldn't trust Him when He asked me to bring my sin into the light. I was only holding back a small percentage, but it made all the difference.

Unless you trust Jesus with everything—100 percent—it shows that you don't really trust Him at all. I may have been calling Him the Lord of my life, but by picking and choosing in what areas I wanted to trust Him based on my own feelings, I was still controlling the relationship. I was functioning as my own lord.

The more I look at the Scriptures, the more I wonder if I was even saved before that moment when I put my full trust in Jesus. I acknowledge that this is an extreme view, but look at it this way: If we are saved by grace *through faith*,[8] and I wasn't fully trusting in Jesus (my faith wasn't in Him), how could I have been saved?

---

8 Ephesians 2:8–9.

I recognize now that my faith was still in my own ability to make the best decisions for my life. By choosing not to trust every word Jesus said, I was trying to pick my own path to salvation and refusing to trust Him about the path He had clearly lined out for me. I was more interested in maintaining my temporary happiness in this world than trusting what Jesus promised would lead to eternal happiness and life. I wanted to receive all the blessings of faith without changing my life or acting in a way that would cause others to label me as odd or extreme. I wanted a relationship with Jesus, but only if I didn't have to risk anything to receive it.

But that's not the life of faith Jesus calls us to. He makes it clear that true faith will change your life in a way that no one can deny. For example, look at a few of the verses that tell us what the everyday life of a Jesus follower will look like:

> Your love for one another will prove to the world that you are my disciples (John 13:35).

> The Holy Spirit produces this kind of fruit in our lives: love, joy, peace, patience, kindness, goodness, faithfulness, gentleness, and self-control (Galatians 5:22–23).

If my faith had been in Christ, then love, kindness, and all the other fruits of the Spirit would have been flowing out of me. Instead, my life was marked by selfishness, apathy, and manipulation. These were not fruits of a Spirit-filled life; they were fruits of a Steve-focused life.

The verse I think concerns me most—because of the possible implications for so many others who are claiming to be followers of Christ but are still functioning as their own lord—is Matthew 7:22–23:

> Many will say to me on that day, "Lord, Lord, did we not prophesy in your name and in your name drive out demons and in your name perform many miracles?" Then I will tell them plainly, "I never knew you. Away from me, you evildoers!" (Matthew 7:22–23 NIV).

Eternal life in heaven is about Who you know, not what you do. I'm sure I would have been one of the guys standing at the gates of heaven with my résumé of all the great things I had done for Jesus. In reality, because I had never trusted Him, I didn't even know Him. I was in church, but I wasn't in Christ. Because I still believed it was my résumé that saved me—all the stuff I supposedly did for Jesus—and I never put my faith in Him, it makes me wonder if I would have been turned away.

Compare all of that to what happened immediately after I chose to trust Jesus fully. Instead of being worried that others would find out about the depth of my addiction, I found myself looking for opportunities to share the story of how Jesus had changed my life. I felt like Peter when the Holy Spirit came upon him and he instantly went from denying his faith to a servant girl to boldly proclaiming Jesus to anyone who would listen.

I felt as if I had a direct line of communication with Jesus and couldn't stop talking to Him. For the first time ever I felt like I had an actual relationship with Him. He wasn't just some imaginary being in my mind; He was the most real and intimate friend I've ever had.

Honestly, I became the crazy Jesus guy, and I wasn't ashamed about it. The change in my life was undeniable and shocking.

And best of all, I've had no doubt whatsoever since that moment that I am saved.[9]

Here's the deal—Jesus makes it absolutely clear that trusting Him will cost you your entire life. There's just no way to be lukewarm and follow Him.[10] Look at the lives of almost every example of faith we see in the Bible. The disciples were all murdered.[11] Paul was tortured, beaten, and eventually killed. Stephen was stoned to death. The list goes on...

But every one of these guys would tell you it was worth it. No matter what trusting Jesus costs you, even if it's your life, it will never compare to the eternal blessing of a relationship with Him.

It's been over three years now since the day I finally trusted Jesus with

---

9 Just to be clear, I'm not saying half the people claiming to be followers of Jesus aren't actually going to heaven at this point. But I will say it's worth asking the tough questions. I'd encourage you to do your own study on this and ask God to show you where your faith really is. If it isn't fully in Jesus, what does that mean for you?

10 Revelation 3:16.

11 Actually, according to church tradition, John was boiled alive and miraculously survived. So technically he wasn't murdered, but I have a feeling he may have wished he had been.

the last remaining areas of my life I had still been trying to control. Accepting responsibility for what I had done cost me my marriage and many of my friends, and it hurt my reputation. But even knowing what I know now, I wouldn't go back to a life of trusting myself instead of trusting Jesus—not for anything. I've since come to understand what Paul was talking about when he wrote this in his letter to the Philippians:

> Yes, everything else is worthless when compared with the infinite value of knowing Christ Jesus my Lord. For his sake I have discarded everything else, counting it all as garbage, so that I could gain Christ (Philippians 3:8).

How Does This Help Me with Porn?

We often think the sin process begins when we find ourselves in front of the computer with our pants around our ankles. But in reality, the process begins much earlier when you stop believing—consciously or unconsciously—that Jesus knows (and wants) what is best for you.

If, however, you can learn to recognize the moment when your trust in Him begins to slip, you can stop the sin process before it ever gets a chance to start.

When I end up losing the battle with pornography, it's a similar process nearly every time. I start thinking about what a life of singleness and celibacy might look like and begin to believe I won't be able to handle it. I decide that Jesus is being unfair by asking me to remain single and is actually holding out on me. I start thinking that my sexual desires are actually sexual *needs,* and that Jesus can't be trusted to meet those needs. It's up to me to meet them.

Notice how all of this happens *before* I ever end up in front of the computer. By the time I even sit down to "check my e-mail" or whatever other excuse I'm trying to convince myself is the real reason I'm there, I've already decided in my mind what is going to happen. I may still go through the motions of trying to resist the temptation, but I've already given myself permission to give in. Fighting it will only increase my anticipation and make it more pleasurable when I eventually give in.

But if I learn to recognize my dwindling trust back when I first start to question Jesus, I can choose to respond with faith and stop this cycle before it even begins. I can trust that He really does know what I need better than I do. I can recognize that I don't need sex to meet my need for intimacy; I don't need a girlfriend or pornography; I only need Jesus.

I can fight the battle of sin by choosing to believe the truth, and the truth will set me free.

If you aren't experiencing the freedom from sin Jesus offers you, ask yourself whether it's a sign that He isn't trustworthy, or a sign that you aren't trusting Him. Don't wait until you *feel* dead to sin or free from bondage before you believe it to be true about you. Trust that it's true because the Bible says it is. If you do choose to trust these truths, you will begin to experience them in your life.

God's goal for your life isn't for you to try to sin less; it's to trust Him more.[12] The amazing thing, though, is the more you trust Him, the less you will end up sinning. This is why life for a believer truly begins when you move from mere belief to absolute, unwavering trust; when you believe that every word Jesus said is true, even for you; when you get in the wheelbarrow on the tightrope; when you jump off the cliff.[13]

So stop playing whack-a-mole with your sin. Trust that Jesus has already set you free from it, and walk away from the game altogether.

Father, I've trusted you with my salvation, but now I'm choosing to trust you with my life as well. I'm choosing to trust that every word you spoke in the Bible is true, whether it feels true or not. I'm choosing to trust that you never make mistakes, which means you will never make a mistake with me. I'm choosing to trust that you always have my best interest in mind, and I recognize that if I knew everything you know, I would make the same decisions for myself. Ultimately, I am choosing to trust that you are who you say you are, and that I am who you say I am.

---

12 Bill Thrall, John Lynch, and Bruce McNicol, *The Cure* (Colorado Springs: NavPress Publishing Group, 2011).

13 Just so you don't think I'm a wuss, I finally did jump off Steelhead Falls. It was awesome!

LIE #8

Holding on to Unforgiveness Has No Effect on My Pornography Addiction

Always forgive your enemies—nothing annoys them so much.

OSCAR WILDE

I was teased quite often as a teenager, so I had a lot of fear about how I would be treated in high school. I wasn't completely pessimistic, though. I had hopes that starting at a new school might provide me with the opportunity to reinvent myself and finally gain popularity. Unfortunately, like many teenagers trying to find their identity through the acceptance of their peers, I believed my best chance for "fitting in" would be with the stoner crowd.

It was the early '90s and the grunge scene was huge in the Northwest, so I tried everything to fit the grunge-rock-stoner identity. I put a Pearl Jam sticker on my school notebook, wore flannel shirts and skate shoes, and attached a chain to my wallet. I even dyed my hair Smurf blue at one point. I may have *looked* like a stoner, but I never did fit in with them. I was what they called a "poser."

Chris, however, was not a poser. He was the coolest kid in the group, and easily the most popular guy with all the stoner girls. For some reason, he seemed to receive great joy from embarrassing and tormenting the less popular kids—including me—in front of the others. I was able to ignore his harassment the majority of the time, but one incident in particular was not so easy for me to forget.

Like on most days, the stoner crowd had congregated around the tables outside of Taco Bell, where they could smoke while eating lunch. This particular day was an especially good day for me because I was sharing a cigarette with the girl I really liked. She was one of the few girls in the group who talked to me and even seemed to genuinely enjoy my friendship, but she was still way out of my league—not that it stopped me from having a huge crush on her. I was feeling much more confidant that day because of the new, limited-edition Nirvana shirt I was wearing. In my teenage logic, I hoped the shirt would finally gain me acceptance into the stoner crowd and maybe even impress the girl.

Partway through lunch, though, Chris came up behind me with a bean burrito, smashed it in my face, and rubbed it all over my new shirt. Everyone saw what happened and began to laugh at me, including the girl. My emotions became so intense in that moment, all I could manage to do was run away as the tears started to flow down my bean-and-cheese-smeared face. It was easily the most embarrassing moment in my life.

Twenty years later, I finally forgave Chris.

What Does Forgiveness Have to Do with Pornography?

You may be wondering why an entire chapter of this book is dedicated to forgiveness. The truth is, forgiveness may be more closely connected to your struggles with pornography than you realize.

The longer you experience freedom from pornography addiction, the better you will become at recognizing Satan's ways of tempting you in that area. Over time, you will become more skilled at recognizing and resisting his attempts to regain that specific foothold in your life. But Satan's goal will always be to keep you trapped in bondage, so if he finds the door to your heart via pornography locked, he will hunt for another point of access. He will look for some part of your life you may not be paying such close attention to. Often, the access he will discover is through unforgiveness.

Which is why it's one of the more common "back doors" he will use to enter your heart and regain a foothold in your life.

> When I forgive whatever needs to be forgiven, I do so with Christ's authority for your benefit, so that Satan will not outsmart us. For we are familiar with his evil schemes (2 Corinthians 2:10–11).

If you believe Satan's lie that unforgiveness has no effect on your spiritual bondage, you will be giving him access back into your life. His presence will compromise your victory in all areas, including your struggles with pornography. This is why having a biblical understanding of forgiveness is critical to your freedom from pornography addiction. You must become aware of his scheme to lure you back into spiritual bondage through unforgiveness, which will grant him easier access to *all* areas of your life.

TRUTH: Unforgiveness is one of the most common ways of allowing spiritual bondage back into your life.

I believe we all understand in some way that forgiveness is important. We read about it all throughout the Bible, we hear our pastors encouraging us to do it, and now, you've got me sitting here telling you the same thing. The problem, though, is many of us have accepted a cheap substitute for forgiveness that keeps us from experiencing the freedom of true, biblical forgiveness. We believe forgiveness is simply saying the right words—or deciding in our heads to forgive. We assume these rituals have fulfilled our forgiveness requirement and call them good enough.

But if that was really forgiveness, why is your heart still full of anger toward your offender? If you are honest, you will probably find that your heart was never on board with the decision to forgive, which means the words or thoughts never reflected any real change within you.

Just like any other area of "good works," your motivation is key. Are you forgiving your offender because you think you *should*, or because it's something you truly *desire* to do? If your motivation is nothing more than *should*, your thoughts toward them will never change. If you've ever had thoughts such as *I forgave you, but I still hate you,* it's a good sign that your forgiveness for that person is motivated by *should*. However, when your forgiveness is motivated by the honest desire of your heart, it changes everything—including you. Instead of praying for your offender to contract an incurable and painful rash, you will want to pray for their well-being. Your deepest desire will no longer be for revenge, but for them to be made right with God.

There's just one problem with all of this, though: You can't just make your heart come on board with the idea of forgiving someone who has hurt you deeply. It's not humanly possible. In fact, none of us are strong enough to even forgive at all, let alone *want* to forgive. But God never expected you to do this with your own power. Remember, if you are in Christ, you've got His love flowing through you, and it's His love that will enable you to truly forgive from your heart. In the same way that "we love because He first loved us,"[1] we can forgive because He first forgave us.

In order for this to happen, you will need to approach forgiveness in the same way Jesus modeled for us on the cross.[2] You will need to forgive your offender before God ("vertical forgiveness") before you ever attempt to forgive them directly ("horizontal forgiveness").

Vertical Forgiveness Must Precede Horizontal Forgiveness

If you don't understand forgiveness as a two-step process, you will see horizontal forgiveness as an isolated decision. You will try to force yourself to forgive your offenders out of duty, with clenched teeth and hate-filled eyes...and it will show. You will say you forgive and move on with your life, but the bitterness will still be festering in your heart. The pain of your past will not go away.

When you forgive your offender before God, though, it will result in a legitimate change in your heart. The bondage that came with your unforgiveness is lifted, freeing you from your anger and bitterness toward them. By trusting God to handle the situation for you, you are released from the need to seek your own justice and will finally be able to approach

1 1 John 4:19,

2 Luke 23:34.

your offender free from any desires for retribution, thoughts of revenge, or demands for restitution. Best of all, your focus will shift off your problem and onto God's promise, empowering you to offer the same forgiveness to your offender that Christ offered to you.

This is a lot to take in, so let's take a deeper look at how each one of these benefits of forgiveness tends to play out.

Vertical Forgiveness Frees You from the Bondage of Bitterness

I'm no expert on the wine-making process, but I do understand the basic concept. You take some grapes, put them in a sealed barrel, and eventually they ferment and become wine. In the same way, if you hold on to unforgiveness in your heart and never release it to God, it will ferment into anger. Furthermore, if you ignore either the wine or your anger for too long, it will become unpalatable. The wine will become vinegar, and your anger will turn into bitterness.[3]

This path to bitterness usually follows a similar pattern regardless of the offense:

- Someone hurts you. It wasn't fair. You did nothing to deserve it, but it still happened.
- You keep replaying the offense over and over in your mind, reliving the pain every time.
- You come to dread any moment where you might be in the same zip code as your offender, let alone the same room.
- You begin looking for opportunities to bring the "true character" of your offender to light, soiling their reputation in an attempt to bolster your own.
- You start telling your side of the story to others, hoping they will agree that you are justified in your growing anger. Perhaps they will even join "your team."

3 I recognize this isn't a perfect analogy because wine is usually considered a good thing, but technically, alcohol is a toxin, so work with me here.

Meanwhile, your anger (and the pain) doesn't go away. It keeps getting more intense. Each time you bring up the offense, either in your mind or by sharing it with others, it's as if you dump another gallon of lighter fluid onto the flames of your bitterness. Eventually, all of your relationships begin to suffer damage from this wildfire raging within your heart:

- Your default response to the optimism of others is to share the sad stories of your miserable life.
- You become the person whose very presence sucks the life out of the room.
- Spending time with you starts to become difficult for others, perhaps even undesirable.
- The anger continues to inflame your heart, crippling your ability to love anyone.
- You become so afraid of getting hurt again that you lose the ability to trust others.
- Instead of being alive and full of joy, you become an isolated, angry, depressed shell of who you once were.

Worst of all, your offender doesn't seem to be hurting at all. In fact, their life appears to be moving along just fine. But that's the problem with bitterness and unforgiveness. You hold onto the offense as if it will somehow hurt your offender. But in reality, it's your own heart that suffers. As the old saying goes, "Bitterness is swallowing poison and hoping the other person dies."

Anger, unforgiveness, bitterness—whatever you want to call them, they're all similar points along the same spectrum. If you allow any one of them to fester within you, you are leaving the door to your heart wide open for more bondage to come in.

> "Don't sin by letting anger control you." Don't let the sun go down while you are still angry, for anger *gives a foothold to the devil* (Ephesians 4:26–27).

As with any addiction, what starts as a seemingly small decision to hold on to an offense will have you locked in shackles before you even recognize what is happening. Thankfully, though, if we read a few verses further, we will see that God has given us a solution to set us free from the chains of bitterness:

> Get rid of all bitterness, rage, anger, harsh words, and slander, as well as all types of evil behavior. Instead, be kind to each other, tenderhearted, forgiving one another, just as God through Christ has forgiven you (Ephesians 4:31–32).

The Greek word used here for forgiveness is *aphiemi*, which literally means, "to hurl away, to release, to free yourself." So forgiving someone isn't setting *them* free—it's setting *yourself* free. It's removing the chains of bondage from *your* heart, not theirs. When you look at it that way, you can see how forgiveness really is God's antidote for bitterness.

Vertical Forgiveness Frees You from Acting as Your Own Judge

If you've ever used a compass, you're familiar with true north and magnetic north. For those of you who have only used the fancy GPS app on your iPhone to navigate the wilderness, though, I'll fill you in.

The needle on a compass works by pointing toward magnetic north, which is somewhere in the Arctic Ocean just north of Canadian territory. True north, however, is geographic north: the direction toward the North Pole. This means the further you are to the east or west, the more "off" your compass is from what your map says is north. In order to compensate for this, you rotate a ring on the compass a specific amount based on where you are. This is called declination. Once it's set, true north and magnetic north will line up and the compass will be accurate. If you fail to adjust for this difference, though, it will cause you all sorts of navigation problems. When you're off by a few degrees and walk a mile, you may only be a hundred feet or so from your intended destination. If, however, you walk 20 miles with an incorrect compass, you had better know the number for your local search-and-rescue crew, because you're going to be way off course.

A similar thing happens in your heart when you allow your view of God to shift away from what is true. When you believe a lie about His character, your focus is no longer pointing directly to Him. It's pointing somewhere off to the side. It may be subtle at first, but the longer you walk down that road, the further deceived you will become. Unforgiveness changes your view of Him in this way because it causes you to view Him as against you rather than for you. And one of the quickest ways someone comes to that conclusion is by moving themselves into the position of judge and jury over those who have offended them.

When you refuse to forgive someone, whether you realize it or not, you stop trusting God to take care of you. You believe the lie that you need to control the situation, act as your own judge, and pursue justice on your own. You are telling God that you know how to handle the situation better than He does, and that your interpretation of justice is more righteous than His.

It's tempting to hear something like that and automatically assume it doesn't apply to you. But before you write this section off, I'd encourage you to consider if you've ever had thoughts such as these:

- *I'm not going to deal with my issues until God deals with my offender. I at least deserve that.*
- *What my offender did was inexcusable. They don't deserve forgiveness so I'm not going to give it to them.*
- *I forgave them the first 20 times they hurt me, but not anymore. Enough is enough.*
- *It isn't fair. If I have to suffer, I want them to suffer as well.*

Chances are, you've thought something along those lines at least once. I know I have. It's normal and common, but that doesn't make it right. If you start to go down this road and pursue justice on your own, it will only pull your view of God further away from the truth of Scripture. You will become so frustrated with what you perceive as a lack of justice that you will begin to wonder if He isn't just against you, but is actually on your offender's team. I must warn you, though—if you walk down this road far enough, you are likely to stop trusting Him altogether.

So what does Scripture say about fairness and justice? Well, God calls us to deal with our own lives and trust Him for justice when it comes to dealing with others.[4] Jesus tells us we have the ability to forgive repeatedly, even when it isn't deserved.[5] We are warned that our lives won't be fair, and as believers we will suffer unjustly at times. But we are also promised that we'll be rewarded for our suffering in eternity.[6] Ultimately, we are told that God is just, and He will make all things right in His timing.[7]

Does your offender deserve forgiveness? No. None of us do. But that didn't stop God from sending Jesus to purchase your forgiveness with His life. And the same cross that covers all the sin you commit also covers all of the sin done *to you*. Furthermore, if your offender comes to Jesus and repents, God forgives their sin as well. All of it. Even what they did to you.

> Let's look at it this way. If somebody sins against me and that person repents, God forgives them. If I refuse to forgive them, can you think how ghastly that is in the sight of God? God is not obligated to forgive that person. That person has sinned against God, and God has never sinned against anybody. Here I am—a person who is a sinner refusing to forgive other sinners while God, who is sinless, is willing to forgive. Have you ever stopped to think about the arrogance that's in me when I refuse to forgive somebody that God has forgiven?[8]

Only God knows the full story, the story from both sides. You don't know the other person's hurts or their baggage. You don't know their thoughts or the condition of their heart at the time. There's probably a reason why they acted the way they did. No, that doesn't make it right or justify it at all, but it can have an effect on the appropriate consequence. Since you don't know those details, you can't be a fair judge. Only God is qualified to judge your offender fairly. It's His job, not yours. Your job is to trust Him to hold them accountable and to bring His justice in His timing.

---

4 Romans 12:19.

5 Matthew 18:21–22.

6 1 Peter 2:20.

7 2 Thessalonians 1:6,

8 R.C. Sproul, *Tough Questions with RC Sproul* (blog), 07 23 2013, www.biblegateway.com/devotionals/tough-questions-with-rc-sproul/2013/07/23.

Vertical Forgiveness Frees You to Walk in Obedience

When you hold on to unforgiveness, your focus remains on your problems. And when your focus is on your problems, it can't be on God's promises. Furthermore, whatever you choose to focus on will significantly influence the path of your life. If you focus on your problems, your life will feel empty and frustrating. If you focus on God's promises, though, you will experience all the amazing benefits He assures you will come from trusting Him. His promises for you are the same whether you obey Him or not, which means forgiving others has nothing to do with your eternal salvation. It does, however, have everything to do with how much you experience His blessing today.

When you decide to forgive someone before God, you are choosing to trust that His promises really are big enough to cover your problem. You are trusting that He will take care of you and that He truly does have your best interest in mind. You're resting in the truth that no matter how hard or painful your life gets, He is in control.

Ultimately, vertical forgiveness is putting your focus back on God, allowing you to seek His will for your life rather than your own. It frees you to walk in obedience to Him.

Isn't There a Verse that Says if We Don't Forgive Others, God Won't Forgive Us?

You're thinking of Matthew 6:14–15:

> If you forgive those who sin against you, your heavenly Father will forgive you. But if you refuse to forgive others, your Father will not forgive your sins (Matthew 6:14–15).

There's an important distinction that is often overlooked about this verse: Jesus spoke it *before* the cross. The once-for-all forgiveness of sin that Jesus purchased for us on the cross had not happened yet.

Today, though, we are living *after* the cross and our sins *have been* forgiven. Look at what these verses, which were written to believers living after the cross, say about forgiveness:

Remember, the Lord *forgave* you, so you must forgive others (Colossians 3:13).

...just as God through Christ *has forgiven* you (Ephesians 4:32).

Anytime we see a reference to forgiveness after the cross, it's past tense. The moment you put your faith in Christ, you were forgiven *fully*,[9] *freely*,[10] and *forever*.[11] The forgiveness you received from Jesus will never change, regardless of your level of obedience.

Lies We Believe About Forgiveness

Hopefully you are beginning to develop a picture of what vertical forgiveness looks like. But before we look at how we actually go about forgiving someone in this way, we first need to look at three lies that people commonly believe about forgiveness—and replace them with the truth. If you don't address these lies, they are likely to become barriers in your mind that will keep you from moving forward.

1. Forgiveness Does Not Require You to Forget the Offense

Chances are you've heard the phrase "God forgives and forgets." There's just one problem with it, though. It's not true. You see, God is omniscient, which means He knows everything—past, present, and future. By definition, this means He is incapable of forgetting *anything*. If He did, He would no longer know the entire past, which means He would no longer be omniscient.

What is true, though, is when God forgives us for an offense He chooses to no longer connect the offense to us in His mind. He knows it happened, but He promises not to hold it against us or bring it up ever again. Likewise, when we forgive others, we are not expected to forget what happened. Honestly, that will never happen. If something requires your forgiveness, it has likely impacted your life in a way you will never fully forget. What we

9 Romans 8:1.

10 Ephesians 2:8–9.

11 Romans 8:38–39.

can do is decide to no longer hold on to the offense. We can choose to live our lives as if it never happened, even though we know full well that it did.

One of the easiest places to see this idea play out is in long-lasting, healthy marriages. These marriages don't survive for decades because two people somehow figured out a way to never hurt one another. They survive because both people continually choose to forgive each other whether it's deserved or not. Instead of becoming bitter and bringing up past offenses, they respond to one another with grace and move forward. They choose to put the health of the relationship above their own self-interest.

This is not the same as ignoring what happened and hoping it will just go away. It's choosing to hand the offense over to God and trusting Him to take care of it, which will allow you to move on with your life free from the bondage that would come if you held on to it.

Now, if the offense is something major, such as abuse, abandonment, or infidelity, the process may not be so easy as simply forgiving your offender and continuing on in the relationship as if the hurt never happened. Which brings us to the next point.

2. Forgiveness Does Not Require You to Blindly Trust Your Offender

Just because you forgive someone doesn't mean you have to trust them right away. Forgiveness is a gift you offer for free—but trust must always be earned. You can forgive an unfaithful spouse for their adultery and still set up boundaries to protect the relationship. Hopefully, you will recognize a growing pattern of trustworthiness in your offender, allowing you to trust them again with small things before you trust them in the larger areas. It is possible that your offender will never become trustworthy, however, in which case the wise decision would be to keep the boundaries in place.

3. Forgiveness Does Not Require You to Tolerate Sin

Likewise, forgiving someone doesn't mean you have to tolerate their sin. If the offense is illegal, you can forgive and still call the police. If the offense is violent, you can separate yourself from the relationship to ensure your safety. Forgiveness never requires you to ignore wisdom or safety in your relationships. Yes, God's desire is always for reconciliation, but He also knows that reconciliation is only possible if there is repentance in both parties.[12] If your offender refuses to repent and continues to exhibit the same hurtful behavior, you may need to remove yourself from the relationship.

Ideally, though, you would be able to pursue a restored relationship with your offender. If you decide you do need to step away, I encourage you to continue to pray for their repentance and look for signs of change in their life. As much as it depends on you, keep pursuing the hope of reconciliation. After all, nothing models the power of the gospel more than the restoration of a hopelessly broken relationship.

So, How Do I Forgive?

There is no official step-by-step guide for how to approach biblical forgiveness. As in many things, God wants to walk through it with you personally rather than just giving you the entire map up front. Yes, the basic process is the same for all occasions—you must first forgive your offender vertically before you forgive them horizontally—but the specific steps will be between you and God.

That being said, the following is a set of seven steps that has helped me navigate this process. Don't consider these to be set in stone—they're simply an example. Seek God's wisdom and ask Him to walk you down the best path for your specific situation.

1. Ask God to Show You Who You Need to Forgive

Set aside some time and get alone with God. Ask Him to bring to mind anyone you might need to forgive. Some of these will be obvious, and some maybe not so much. Either way, write them all down. Trust that any offense that comes to mind is from Him. After all, it's better to have extra names on your list than to ignore one you decide is inconsequential.

Once you have your list of names, start writing specific offenses by each one. Try to be as thorough as possible, listing not only the offense but any ancillary effects as well. For instance, I knew I needed to forgive Chris for

---

12 Romans 12:18.

embarrassing me publicly, but I also needed to forgive him for damaging my social status, adding another wound to my already low view of myself, and even the expense of a ruined shirt.

2. Recognize the Pain these Offenses Have Caused You

Before you can truly forgive someone, it's important to understand deep down the full extent of what you're forgiving them for. In order to do that, you must acknowledge and recognize all your feelings and emotions connected to each offense.

As you go through your list, pause on each offense and reconnect with all the feelings you associated with it—both today and in the past. It's possible that you may have buried or ignored many of these feelings, hoping they would go away. If that is the case, now is the time to dig them back up, bring them into the light, and allow God to help you deal with them.

Again, be thorough. Don't try to ignore certain emotions such as anger, hatred, or bitterness, because you consider them to be sinful emotions. Don't try to downplay feelings such as betrayal or abandonment because you think they are signs of weakness. The purpose of this step isn't to analyze your emotions; it's to uncover them.

As I looked back at the burrito incident, I realized there were a lot of emotions I experienced but never recognized consciously. The embarrassment was obvious, but there was also shame from believing I deserved it, betrayal when my friends laughed at me, and the ongoing fear of what Chris might to do to me next.

3. Acknowledge Your Feelings to God

The first step in vertical forgiveness is to acknowledge all of your feelings, emotions, and pain to God. Go through your list and tell Him how much the offense hurt, how much hatred you still have in your heart toward your offender, and how unfair it all was. For some of you, this may be a silent time of reflection through prayer. For others, it may involve going somewhere remote like a cabin and screaming them out loud to God.

You know you can do that, right? It really is okay to vent your frustration to God, even if it involves screaming. Look at the first part of Psalm 43:

Clear my name, God; stick up for me
against these loveless, immoral people.
Get me out of here, away
from these lying degenerates.
I counted on you, God.
Why did you walk out on me?
Why am I pacing the floor, wringing my hands
over these outrageous people? (Psalm 43:1–2 MSG)

Does this sound like a quiet and reserved request to God? Not at all. I imagine the psalmist looking up to the sky, shouting, "WHY ARE YOU LETTING THIS HAPPEN? I DON'T DESERVE THIS! IT'S NOT FAIR!" The Psalms are full of examples such as this, showing us that it's okay to pour our hearts out to God. He can take it. He *wants* to take it.

4. Hand the Offense Over to God

If you continue reading in Psalm 43, you can recognize this handoff when the psalmist stops focusing on his problem and puts his focus back onto the promises of God:

Why are you down in the dumps, dear soul?
Why are you crying the blues? Fix my eyes on God—
soon I'll be praising again. He puts a smile on my face.
He's my God (Psalm 43:5).

Tell God that you no longer want to hold on to the offense and ask Him to remove its chains from your heart. Tell Him you believe the cross has set you free from all sin—even the sins that were done against you—and that you are now choosing to walk in that freedom. Tell Him you trust Him to bring justice to all things in His timing. Most importantly, tell Him you're choosing to forgive your offender for the specific offense, and you trust Him to change your heart toward them.

5. Forgive Your Offender Directly

After you have forgiven your offender before God, you are finally free to forgive them directly. But just because you are *free* to forgive doesn't mean you will automatically *feel* like forgiving. Horizontal forgiveness will more than likely still be an extreme battle of your will. If you trust God and do what He asks of you, though, your heart will quickly come on board.

How this looks specifically will be different for each situation, which is why it's important to seek God's wisdom every time. You may feel led to contact your offender, offer forgiveness, and possibly even seek reconciliation, which was the path I felt the Lord calling me to with Chris. I sent him a letter explaining how the events of that day affected me negatively for many years. I wasn't angry or condemning, but I was honest. I told him about the freedom I had found in Christ, and how that freedom has allowed me to finally forgive him. A few days later, he responded back and thanked me for the letter. I could tell he had come to realize how hurtful some of his actions in the past had been and was dealing with some guilt because of that. I hope that my forgiveness helped to set him free from at least a portion of his guilt.

What if your offender has passed away? Or perhaps they are around, but it is not safe or wise for you to contact them. In cases such as these, it may be beneficial to imagine them sitting across from you in an empty chair and visualize having the conversation with them. This will allow you to continue with the forgiveness process even if your offender is not able or willing to be a part of it. If you seek God's wisdom and guidance, He will make clear to you whether His way involves contacting your offender directly or not.

6. Trust God's Promise that Forgiveness Sets You Free

Don't be too surprised if it feels as though forgiveness hasn't changed anything between you and your offender. It's possible that he may remain unrepentant and continue to hurt you. Remember, though, forgiveness isn't about changing your offender or even fixing the relationship. As I mentioned above, reconciliation may not be possible. Rather, forgiveness is about freeing you from the offense. And the beautiful thing about forgiveness is it will never stop bringing freedom. It's the "out" that God gives you to protect you from the sins of others against you. So each time you are hurt, hand the offense over to Him and you will be freed from it. It's His promise to you, and you can trust it.

7. Recognize How God Has Changed Your Heart

When I look back to my high-school days, I no longer see how much Chris hurt me. I see how much he was hurting. Things I never noticed before—like his last name changing several times over the four years I knew him—stand out as clues to the hard reality of his life back then. Chris wasn't the bully because he was a jerk. He was the bully because his heart was broken and he didn't know how to handle those emotions. The fact I now recognize these things proves to me that God has truly changed my heart toward Chris.

I encourage you to look for these types of changes in your own heart as well. The more you recognize them as proof that God has changed your heart, the easier it will be to trust Him again when He calls you to forgive in the future.

Remember, Christ has set you free from bondage, so why would you walk right back into it? When someone hurts or offends you, you always have a choice. You can take the path of unforgiveness, which leads to bitterness and bondage, or you can take the path of forgiveness, leading you to freedom.

The choice may be obvious, but it's never easy. In fact, offering forgiveness will more than likely be one of the hardest things God ever asks you to do.

> The moment the focus of your life shifts from your badness to His goodness and the question becomes not "What have I done?" but "What can He do?" release from remorse can happen; miracle of miracles, you can forgive because you are forgiven, accept because you are accepted, and begin to start building up the very places you once tore down. There is grace to help in every time of trouble. That grace is the secret to being able to forgive. Trust it.[13]

13 John R. Claypool, "Learning to Forgive Ourselves," in *Best Sermons 1* (San Francisco: Harper & Row, 1988), 269.

You may never be strong enough to forgive. But you've got the power of Christ within you. And His power is *always* more than enough.

Father, I am choosing today to forgive those who have offended me and to hand the offenses over to you. Please free me from any bondage or bitterness that I've allowed into my life through my unforgiveness. I will trust you to be my vindicator from now on, releasing me from the need to act as judge on my own. You have promised that you will always have my best interest in mind, and I will trust that promise even when my life seems unfair or unjust. Please soften my heart toward those who have hurt me in the past, as well as those who will hurt me in the future. Thank you that the cross has set me free from all sin, even these sins that were committed against me.

LIE #9

I Must Shut Down My Desires if I Want to Be Free from Pornography

I used to desire many, many things, but now I have just one desire, and that's to get rid of all my other desires.

JOHN CLEESE

I used to be a marathon runner. At least that's what I called myself. Technically I hadn't run a marathon yet, but I was training for one, so that was good enough to earn me the label as far as I was concerned.

I didn't actually enjoy waking up before sunrise to run, but I kept doing it because I had a deeper desire driving me. I desired to cross the finish line of the Portland Marathon, arms raised high in victory, reveling in the celebratory atmosphere with all the other "elite" runners. Someday, years down the road, I pictured my grandkids climbing up on my lap, pointing to my medal hanging on the wall, and asking me, "Grandpa, tell us about the time you ran a marathon!"[1]

Now, there wasn't anything inherently wrong with my training to run a marathon. The question I needed to ask myself was, what was my real desire for doing so? If I had stopped to take an honest look at what was

1 You can see it coming already, can't you? This is the part of the book where I mention Hebrews 12:1 and encourage you to run a good race for Jesus. This isn't one of those books. Sorry.

driving me to run, I would have recognized that my desire wasn't just to finish a marathon, it was to achieve an identity I could be proud of. I wanted to be someone who accomplished something special. These were desires running could never fulfill, though. But because I had allowed these desires to seize control of my heart, nothing was going to stand in the way of them.

Partway through my marathon training, my wife and daughter and I were in Seattle for a friend's wedding and took the opportunity to stick around a few extra days to camp in Olympic National Park. I'm a meticulous planner, so I mapped out the entire trip and scheduled everything before we ever left town. However, I'd never thought to ask my wife what she wanted to do. I was only concerned with my own desires, so I ended up planning our entire trip around my weekend "long run."[2]

My plan was for us to spend Friday night at the Hoh River campground so I could wake up at sunrise and run the Hoh River trail. I had been dreaming about hiking this trail for years, so it seemed like the perfect opportunity to check it out. Once we pulled into the parking lot, though, my heart sank. The campground was closed for repaving.

I wish I could say I handled the situation well. The truth is, my response exposed how addicted I was to my own self-centered desires.

I parked the car and went into the ranger station to make sure there wasn't some mistake. No matter how much I embarrassed my wife by yelling at the girl at the desk and lecturing her about how this was messing up my plans, nothing changed. The campsite was closed. No exceptions. The trail, however, was still open.

The ranger directed us to another campsite about 15 miles down the road, where we eventually set up for the night. I wasn't about to admit defeat, though. I told my wife I'd just leave earlier and drive to the trailhead. I'd get my run in and still be back in time for breakfast. She graciously pointed out to me that I was asking if I could abandon her and our daughter in some remote campsite along the side of a highway.

---

2 For those who aren't familiar with marathon training, it generally consists of a 3- to 5-mile run most mornings and a "long run" on the weekend that increases in distance with each week.

My misplaced desire had blinded me to the selfishness of what I was asking, so I continued to plead with her. I *had* to run the Hoh trail!

Out of frustration, she eventually agreed to wake up early, pack up camp, and drop me off at the trailhead so I could get my run in. This also meant she would have nothing to do for three hours, but I hadn't bothered to think through that. I'd found a way to run the trail, which was all that mattered to me. As it turned out, she drove an hour each way to the nearest town to get coffee while our daughter, who should have still been asleep, fussed in the back seat. I'm sure it was as enjoyable as it sounds.

Yeah, I got my run in, but at what cost? My actions proved to my wife that my desire to be a marathon runner was more important to me than being a good husband or father. Years later, when we were trying to work through our wounds in counseling, she mentioned that very trip as the moment she had started to question whether she regretted marrying me.

Friends, this is why it is so important that you learn to recognize the power of your desires and seek to understand how they are affecting your life.

The Power of Your Desires

God has placed *desire* within everyone's heart. It's arguably one of the most powerful and driving forces we can experience. As John Eldredge says, nothing good ever happens without the motivation of desire:

> [Desire] is the essence of the human soul, the secret of our existence. Absolutely nothing of greatness happens without it. Not a symphony has been written, a mountain climbed, an injustice fought, or a love sustained apart from desire. Desire fuels our search for the life we prize.[3]

Desire is a good thing, but like many of the things that God has intended for good, it can be abused. Satan understands this of course, which is why he is constantly trying to hijack your heart's desires. He will entice you

3 John Eldredge, *The Journey of Desire* (Nashville: Thomas Nelson Inc., 2000). I owe many of the ideas of this chapter to this amazing book. I can't recommend it enough. I encourage you to pick up a copy and dig much deeper into your understanding of desire, as this chapter only scratches the surface compared to Eldredge's work.

with things you *think* you desire. But in reality, these things are only distracting you from recognizing what you *truly* desire:

> The option we have chosen is to reduce our desire to a more manageable size. We allow it only in small doses—just what we can arrange for. Dinner out, a new sofa, a vacation to look forward to, a little too much to drink. It's not working. The tremors of the earthquake inside are beginning to break out.[4]

When we accept these cheap substitutes, though, our deepest desires don't just go away. They may sit dormant for years, but eventually, like magma underneath a volcano, they will explode through the surface. And when that happens, they rarely appear as an outpouring of righteous desire. They're much more likely to erupt as an all-night porn binge, an angry tirade, or an affair.

When we experience these types of eruptions in our lives, we tend to blame them on having too much desire. We wonder if the best path to holiness, maturity, and sanctification is to shut down our desire completely—to overcome it. We buy into the lie that we must kill—or at least minimize—our desire if we ever wish to find freedom from future explosions.

But in order to shut down your desire, you would need to shut down your heart. The two always go hand in hand. Once you shut down your heart, there's a problem. You can no longer offer it to anyone—not to your wife, not to your kids, not even to God. You will become a man without passion…a man without purpose…a man who only exists to fulfill his obligations.

Ugh. Where is the life in that?

It often feels like there is no good solution. We fear that our desire will grow out of control and explode, but we also fear shutting it down will castrate us. And rightfully so. So what options do we have?

The best option, as always, is to seek to understand the truth about your desires. And the truth is this: God doesn't want you to shut them down or even try to overcome them. He wants to redeem the desires of your heart so He can use them for the good of His kingdom.

4 Eldredge, *The Journey of Desire.*

TRUTH: God doesn't want you to shut down your desires. He wants to redeem them for His good.

Desire certainly has the potential to lead you into sin, but it also has the potential to transform you once it has been redeemed. As we saw with King David, his desire led to his affair with Bathsheba, but it was that same desire—once it had been redeemed—that allowed him to write so many wonderful, passionate psalms, many of which we still sing today.

Look again at the parable of the lost son. His desires led him into a life of sin, rebellion, and blatant debauchery. But the same desire that drew him toward sin led him back to his father once he "came to his senses."[5] Meanwhile, the older brother shows us the danger of shutting down our desire: ending up with a life motivated only by duty. Yes, it kept him in line—to our knowledge he never had any weeklong benders in Vegas—but it also kept him from experiencing a meaningful relationship with his father. In the end, which brother ended up in the loving embrace of the father and which brother chose not to enter the party?

You may be tempted, like the older brother, to shut down your desires as an attempt at living a holy life. But Jesus calls you to embrace them so you can come alive. Remember, Jesus didn't come to offer you more duties—He came to offer you life![6]

But What if My Desires are Sinful?

If you ask the question "What if my desires are sinful?" it's only fair to also consider the implications if the opposite is true. What if your desires *aren't* sinful? What if they have been redeemed? What if, the moment you put your faith in Jesus, your desires were changed from sinful to righteous? What if the deepest desires of your heart are actually good?

Your Desires Have Been Redeemed

I heard a story of a man who knew looking at porn was wrong but couldn't find a way to stop. He went to ask his pastor what he thought he should do.

5 Luke 15:17.

6 John 10:10.

After a short moment of thought, the pastor looked him in the eyes and told him, "Do whatever you want."

"Wait, I don't think I heard that correctly. You said do whatever I want."

"Yep. I think you should do whatever you want," his pastor said once again.

"But what if I want to look at porn?" questioned the man.

"If you want to look at porn, then go ahead and look at porn."

The man couldn't believe what he was hearing. After going back and forth with the pastor like this for a minute or so he finally got frustrated and yelled, "But I don't want to look at porn!"

His pastor just smiled and said "Exactly."

You're in the same boat, aren't you? You may sense a desire to look at porn from time to time, but it isn't the deepest desire of your heart. It's not coming from the *real* you. The real you wants nothing to do with it. The real you hates porn. If you truly desired pornography, you wouldn't be spending your time reading this book, would you? Whether you realize it yet or not, if you are in Christ, your heart's desires have already been redeemed.

Remember Paul's struggle with sin in Romans 7? He recognized that it wasn't he himself who was producing these evil desires in him; it was the sin that dwelled in his flesh. He even admitted that he hated the sin and didn't want to give into it. He understood that his flesh, and the sinful desires that came along with it, was not who he really was. He chose to believe the truth of the revelation God had given him—which he wrote down as inspired Scripture—and based his identity solely on his position in Christ. He understood that the truest thing about him was that Jesus had resurrected his heart. And because the Holy Spirit now dwelled in his *new* heart, his deepest desires were aligned with God's desires.

Paul understood that his new heart was the fulfillment of a prophecy written by Ezekiel hundreds of years earlier:

> I will give you a new heart, and I will put a new spirit in you. I will take out your stony, stubborn heart and give you a tender, responsive heart. And I will put my Spirit in you so that

> you will follow my decrees and be careful to obey my regulations (Ezekiel 36:26–27).

Paul realized that God's desire was not that he try to change his heart's desires. Paul knew his heart's desires had already been changed!

> This means that anyone who belongs to Christ *has become* a new person. The old life is gone; a new life *has begun!* (2 Corinthians 5:17).

Just like Paul, the moment you put your faith in Christ, you were given a new heart—a redeemed heart with redeemed desires. This means you are no longer a hard-hearted, self-centered seeker of sin. You are a holy and righteous temple for the Spirit of Christ. Your heart's deepest desires are for the things of God.

Furthermore, because the Spirit of Christ dwells within your redeemed heart, you now have the power to live your life like Jesus, as William Temple tells us:

> It's no good giving me a play like Hamlet or King Lear and telling me to write a play like that. Shakespeare could do it; I can't. And it is no good showing me a life like the life of Jesus and telling me to live a life like that. Jesus could do it; I can't. But if the genius of Shakespeare could come and live in me, then I could write plays like his. And if the Spirit of Jesus could come and live in me, then I could live a life like his.

Once you start to believe this truth about your redeemed heart, you will recognize some pretty amazing changes happening in your life. Instead of looking at sin and thinking, *I can't do this* or *I shouldn't do this,* you will respond with thoughts like *I don't do that anymore,* or *That's no longer who I am.* Instead of resisting temptation out of a sense of duty, you will recognize that you are avoiding it because your heart no longer desires it.

Your new heart also won't desire to get away with anything. Before I trusted Christ, I was constantly looking for ways to cover up my sinful desires. But now, instead of trying to get away *with* sin, my desire is to get away *from* sin.

For example, take my views on premarital sex. I always claimed I wanted to save sex for marriage. In reality, I was only attempting to remain pure because of a sense of moral duty. But now, I view sex outside of marriage as an inherently selfish act. If I were dating a woman, pursuing her sexually would be choosing to give in to the lust within my flesh while ignoring her spiritual well-being. I would be leading her into bondage in exchange for a few moments of physical pleasure. What we might call "making love" would in fact be the exact opposite. If I truly loved her, I would make her protection my highest priority. Now, instead of desiring to see how close to the line we could get without giving in, I desire to protect us both by setting safe boundaries far away from anything that may lead us toward temptation.

It might seem easy for me to say all this now while I'm single and not dating, but I honestly believe this is how I would respond if I were in a relationship. And how can I say that? Because I believe this change in perspective is proof that God truly has redeemed the desires of my heart.

What is the Deepest Desire of Your Heart?

John D. Rockefeller was one of the wealthiest men in the world in his day. The story's been told many times that he was asked, "How much money will be enough?" His response? "Just a little bit more." Even with more money than he could ever spend in his lifetime, he still wanted more. He must have sensed that some desire within him was still unfulfilled. But instead of considering if the way he was attempting to meet that desire wasn't actually working, he bought into a lie: He just needed more of what he was already chasing after to finally be fulfilled.

I see this same idea play out with my daughter. Every time we go to the store, she tells me that the deepest desire of her heart is for another Barbie. She truly believes she will not be happy unless she gets one. I've tried to explain to her that a new Barbie might make her happy for a little while, but the happiness will wear off and the new Barbie will end up in a box collecting dust with the rest of her dolls. I try to explain to her that another Barbie will not make her any happier than the Barbies she already has. Being the wise young lady that she is, her response is usually "Then I must need *lots* of new Barbies!" We can learn a lot about our hearts from five-year-old girls.

Have you ever wondered why the things of this world never seem to fully satisfy your desires? The things we chase after may bring some fulfillment, but it's never lasting. Just like our hunger for food (or porn), we must keep coming back to satisfy our desires again and again. We believe the path to fulfillment must be found in *more.*

But what if there was a way to truly meet the deepest desires of your heart? A way for your heart to never be hungry or thirsty again? A way to shift your mind from *I need more* to *I have more than enough*?

> Jesus declared, "I am the bread of life. Whoever comes to me will never go hungry, and whoever believes in me will never be thirsty" (John 6:35).

The deepest desire of your heart is for *life.* Think about it. If you have no life, what else matters? It's the reason Jesus came to rescue you, to replace your heart of stone with a heart of flesh. To give you life. Your heart needed to be made alive—it *desired* life—and Jesus fulfilled that desire once and for all. This is not just any life, though—it's life that cannot die—eternal life!

But we still have a sense that we aren't quite there yet, don't we? Our hearts may have come alive in Christ, but they are not home. Not yet. If anything, the new life in our hearts makes them all the more prone to breaking when we witness the pain and suffering of this fallen world we live in. It serves as a constant reminder that we were not made for this world; we were made for something better. Our hearts were made for eternal life with Jesus, and every other desire originates from this deepest desire of all.

Your Heart Desires Eternity

Many people simply don't think about eternity at all. They've accepted this world as the ultimate reality—the be-all and end-all of their existence. If you're a follower of Jesus, you've no doubt given it at least some thought. But even then, there's a good chance you are looking at eternity in much the same way as a retirement account. Yeah, you're glad it's there, and someday you will reap the benefits of it. But it's not something you think about on a regular basis. Eternity may be in the back of your mind, but you don't actively desire it. At least you don't realize that you do.

But why is this? If eternal life really is the deepest desire of our hearts, why don't we spend more time thinking about it? Longing for it? Why are we more excited to watch the next football game than we are to spend eternity with Jesus?

Maybe it's because we have an incorrect view of what eternity with Jesus will be like.

Many of us have a vision of heaven based more on Looney Tunes cartoons than Scripture. We believe our eternity will be nothing more than sitting around in togas, strumming harps, and floating on clouds. If we're lucky, maybe we'll get a sweet pair of wings.

Here's the deal: This popular view of our eternal destination is simply not biblical. It is more closely related to Greek mythology than the truth of Scripture. And honestly, it's lame. Which is why no one truly desires it.

Scripture actually tells us quite a bit about our eternal destination, and it's not necessarily where you think it may be. I always assumed when God was finally done with Earth, He was going to blow it up in some cosmic firework display and we'd go on to live forever in a cloud city—probably something similar to the Care Bears' Care-a-lot. But look at what Scripture says:

> Look! I am creating new heavens and a *new earth*,
> and no one will even think about the old ones anymore
> (Isaiah 65:17).

> Then I saw a new heaven and a *new earth*, for the old heaven
> and the old earth had disappeared.
> And the sea was also gone (Revelation 21:1).

Our eternal destination is not somewhere up in the sky; it's on a *new* Earth. In the same way God has redeemed your heart and made it new, He will redeem the Earth and make it new as well. It will be completely restored, free from sin and death and sadness, brought back to its original glory. The things we love about this Earth—mountains, waterfalls, sunsets, beaches—are merely foreshadows of what our eternal destination will be like. They are signposts that God has placed around us to point our hearts toward our real home.

Like He did in the Garden of Eden, God will walk among the people of the new Earth as well. He will establish His holy city on the new Earth and live here with us.[7] We will worship Him, but not just with singing. Our whole lives will be worship. We will be given work to do—work we love, work that makes us come alive. There will be parties and feasts, festivals and food. Anything in this world that makes your heart come alive will be magnified by the glory of God's presence. Take the best day you've ever experienced, multiply it by infinity, and imagine experiencing it for eternity.

That sounds better than strumming a harp all day, doesn't it?

Why am I saying all of this? Because there's only one way you can recognize that the deepest desire of your heart is for eternity: if your vision of eternity is based on the truth. You could hear a hundred times that your heart was made for eternity, but if you don't realize how wonderful it will be, you'd just roll your eyes.

Once you learn the truth about the eternity your heart is longing for, though, nothing will be able to lure your desire away from that vision.[8] As Antoine de Saint-Exupéry said,

> If you want to build a ship, don't drum up the men to gather wood, divide the work, and give orders. Instead, teach them to yearn for the vast and endless sea.

You will long for heaven as sailors long for the sea. Nothing will be able to pull the desires of your heart away from eternity.

Nothing, that is, except forgetting that vision.

Your Flesh Desires That Its Needs Be Met Immediately

If Satan can't convince you to shut down your desires completely, he will try to convince you to give them away to something else. He will look for ways to steal your focus away from eternity by offering you substitutes

---

7 Revelation 21:2.

8 If you want an even deeper understanding of what the Bible teaches us about heaven, I recommend that you read *Heaven* by Randy Alcorn. It completely transformed my understanding of eternity.

to fulfill your desires immediately, replacing the desires of your heart with desires of the flesh. These fleshly desires will distract you, pulling your thoughts away from God and numbing your heart to a point where you forget your deepest desire altogether.

This was the same plan Satan attempted to use on Jesus.[9] Every offer he made to Jesus was an offer of immediate gratification. He was essentially saying, "Jesus, you don't want to wait until heaven to get your desires met. Let me meet them for you right now, in the flesh." But Jesus knew the devil's promises were empty. He knew he could not be trusted. The only way those desires would truly be met was for Him to trust His Father to meet them.

You may never have a serpent tempt you with the keys to a kingdom, but he surely will try to hijack your heart's desire in much the same way. He will offer you ways to fill your life up with so many worldly distractions that you won't have any time left to focus on eternity. If you only look to satisfy the desires of your flesh, the desires of your heart will become weakened... forgotten...far too easily replaced.

> Our Lord finds our desires, not too strong, but too weak. We are half-hearted creatures, fooling about with drink and sex and ambition when infinite joy is offered us, like an ignorant child who wants to go on making mud pies in a slum because he cannot imagine what is meant by the offer of a holiday at the sea. We are far too easily pleased.[10]

We become so distracted by the things of this world that we forget about eternity. As the saying goes, out of sight, out of mind.

We give ourselves away to things that are not our true desires. These substitutes creep into our lives so slowly that we fail to recognize them until their claws have already clutched our hearts. By that point they have become our idols. Perhaps they have even become addictions.

If you never question whether a substitute desire is becoming a distraction, you will blindly accept it as a normal part of life. This is why no one ever recognizes an addiction until it is firmly established. If you want to

---

9 See Matthew 4.

10 C.S. Lewis, *Weight of Glory* (New York: HarperCollins, 2001).

become more aware of these distractions, though, the easiest place to discover them is to look at your calendar. What is consuming the majority of your free time?

- Is your TIVO so full that you must watch an entire season of *Game of Thrones* to free up space?
- Did you just find a guidebook with 50 new trails and feel like you have to hike them all as soon as possible?
- Has a new expansion pack been released, making it absolutely crucial that your wizard earn the Golden Scepter of Orginoth before anyone else?
- Do you find yourself losing track of time while mindlessly surfing the Internet every night?
- Do you spend hours on the treadmill or at the gym while your family constantly wonders where Daddy is?

The way you fill up your free time can tell you a lot about how you are handling your desire.

TV, video games, and hobbies are not always bad things. But if they are distracting you from slowing down long enough to recognize what your heart truly longs for, perhaps they have become distractions. Perhaps these substitute desires of your flesh have crowded out the eternal desires of your heart.

Ultimately, consider this: Have you allowed yourself to become so busy—so distracted by chasing the things of this world—that you haven't stopped to think about what your heart truly desires? Perhaps, much like Rockefeller, you are looking for *more* of what you already have to eventually lead to lasting fulfillment. If the desires you are chasing are based in this world, though, *more* will only lead you further away from experiencing the eternal life your heart desires.

By God's design, there's a simple way to train yourself to become much more aware of these things. It all comes down to a single question you can ask of every desire: *Is this desire contributing to my fulfillment in eternity, or only toward my fulfillment immediately?*

Living with an Eternal Perspective

I recently saw a video of author and speaker Francis Chan giving a wonderful illustration of eternity. He had a rope at least 50 feet long with a small section on one end, about half an inch, colored bright red. The red spot, he explained, represented our entire life here on Earth. The remainder of the rope represented eternity. In reality, the remainder of the rope could stretch to the moon and back and still wouldn't be an adequate representation, but the idea is the same. Our life here on earth is microscopic when we hold it up against the timeline of eternity.

Many of us lack this perspective. So we spend the majority of our energy, passion, and desire focusing on things we believe will make us happy during this tiny sliver of time we call life. We make decisions that benefit us *immediately* rather than considering what will bring the most joy in *eternity*. We're like a child who is offered the choice of a single piece of candy today or an entire box of candy tomorrow. Because small children have no concept of time and are focused only on the present, they will always choose the single piece of candy.

In the same way, if you don't have an eternal perspective when it comes to your desires, you will make decisions that focus only on what you can get today without considering the long-term or eternal consequences. How many affairs, for example, would be avoided if our perspective included more than just our immediate desire? Would both people still go through with it if they fully considered the long-term consequences of the affair on those they loved? Would they still pursue each other if their perspective allowed them to recognize the spiritual bondage and emotional pain that comes from engaging in sexual sin? This is why having an eternal perspective is so vitally important.

Trust your true identity as a child of God. Then your true desires will flow from the Spirit of Christ within you and will always point you toward an eternal perspective. Of course, if you forget your identity and allow yourself to believe you're still a slave to sin, then your desires will shift back to meeting your own needs in the flesh. In a word, living a life of following Jesus all comes down to whether you trust that what God says about you is true.

In order to illustrate this better, let me share with you how I've seen my desires change in the last few years. If you had asked me what my desires were before I came to trust my identity in Christ, I would have responded with my "bucket list."[11] I wanted to climb all the mountains in Oregon (and perhaps even Denali someday). I wanted to through-hike the Pacific Crest Trail. I wanted to make good money so I could retire early to tour the country in an Airstream camper. I wanted to fulfill many other desires that lacked any eternal significance.

These days, my deepest desires no longer revolve around a bucket list. They revolve around eternity. My desire now is to help other men find freedom from pornography addiction and to see their hearts come alive to Christ. I also desire to be the best father I can be, modeling the love of Jesus to my daughter in a way that will help draw her closer to Him. I desire to see my marriage restored so fully that my wife and I might be able to help other couples who are going through struggles similar to those we have endured. Ultimately, I desire my life to be used by God in whatever ways He chooses to use me. Instead of chasing after what makes me happy during this life—the red sliver of the rope—my desires are now focused on the endless length of rope that represents eternity. And the most amazing thing? This eternal perspective has led me to more happiness and fulfillment in this life than anything else.

> Aim at Heaven and you will get Earth thrown in:
> Aim at Earth and you will get neither.[12]

Yes, I still desire to do the things on my bucket list, but they are no longer the deepest desires of my heart. That's why the majority of my free time is now filled with writing and counseling instead of hiking or television. In fact, the pressure to accomplish the things on my list has been eliminated

---

11 A "bucket list" is a list of all the things you want to do before you "kick the bucket." In other words, the stuff you want to accomplish before you die.

12 C.S. Lewis, *Mere Christianity* (New York: HarperCollins, 2001).

because I know I will have all of eternity to get around to them. If I don't get a chance to hike the Pacific Crest Trail before I kick the bucket, I'll just do it on the new Earth, in a redeemed body, sharing a tent with Jesus. How cool is that?

How Does This Help Me with Porn?

I used to love snowshoeing. Nothing made me feel alive like getting out into the snowy wilderness to explore the beauty of God's creation in the winter. Once I got a pair of backcountry skis, though, I suddenly realized how lame snowshoeing really was. Instead of trudging awkwardly down powder-loaded bowls, I now float down them effortlessly. Instead of loading my heavy alpine boots into my pack while trudging up the mountain, I can ascend with my skis on my feet, leaving my climbing boots and snowshoes at home and shaving 15 pounds off my pack load.

If someone had told me I would need to give up snowshoeing before I had discovered backcountry skiing, it would have broken my heart. I would have fought it passionately. But once I discovered something much better, giving it up wasn't even an issue. In fact, I forgot about my snowshoes altogether until recently when I dusted them off to sell them on Craigslist.

The same thing happens when you discover the true desires you are attempting to meet through pornography. Instead of fighting the temptation to look at porn, you will simply forget about it. This sounds too good to be true, but again, isn't that why the gospel is called the good news?

However, in order to do this you will need to do some digging around in your desires. And no one knows the true desires of your heart better than the One who has redeemed your heart. The next time you feel drawn to look at porn, stop for a minute and ask Jesus what your real desire is. What do you, as a new creation in Christ, truly desire? Ask Jesus—He knows.

Often, especially at first, you will find only a fleshly desire driving you to pornography, and that's okay. Recognizing this lack of legitimate desire can still help you see the temptation for what it truly is. Perhaps your desire to look at porn is the sexual equivalent of eating an entire box of Oreos. You're not doing it because you are hungry; you're doing it because you're bored. You don't actually desire food; you just want something to do.

Sometimes you will discover a legitimate desire driving you toward pornography. Remember the needs we talked about back in lie #3—the need for validation as a man, the need for adventure, and the need for intimacy? These are all legitimate needs God has placed in your heart. You may discover your desire to look at pornography is actually an attempt to meet one of these needs immediately rather than trust God to fulfill that need eternally.

This process will be similar to peeling layers off an onion. Each time you go through the exercise of discovering your true desire, you are likely to reveal another layer, bringing you to a deeper understanding of your heart. Over time, you will become more skilled at recognizing your deepest desires. For that reason, I encourage you to practice this process with all of your desires, not just pornography. For example, if I want a new jacket, I ask myself if it's because I truly need it, or because I desire to look outdoorsy. When I post something on Facebook, is it because I truly believe it's worth sharing, or because I desire to be seen as witty or interesting? When you practice the process of uncovering your truest desires in all areas of your life, you become more skilled at discovering what is driving you when it matters the most.

Once you identify your deepest desires, bring them before God and ask Him to give them to you in abundance. You know you can do that, right? Oh yeah. God actually *wants* to bless your desires:

> Take delight in the LORD,
> and he will give you your heart's desires
> (Psalm 37:4).

You must desire the Lord first and foremost to be sure that nothing else becomes an idol. If you trust Him, He will bless your heart and give you its desires. And when He does, move toward them with the same passion you've been dedicating to the desires of your flesh.

A warning: Once your heart gets a taste of its true desires, nothing will ever be the same. You will never again be okay with settling for halfway. But you never wanted to settle anyway, did you? You've always sensed, deep within your heart, that the only thing you've ever truly desired was to be fully alive. John Eldredge says it best:

> Don't ask yourself what the world needs. Ask yourself what makes you come alive. Because what the world needs, is men who have come alive.[13]

The more you come to recognize the true desires of your redeemed heart, the more you will desire the things of God and the less you will desire porn. Your view of pornography will become more in line with God's view. And this will allow you to see it for what it really is. You will begin to see the women in those movies as sisters who are deeply hurt and broken by their own sin and shame, yet deeply loved and pursued by Christ just as you are. Instead of lust, you will start to feel sadness and empathy for them as you more fully recognize their situation. You no longer will see them as sexual objects, but as fellow human beings with broken hearts. Your desires will shift from objectifying them to praying for them. The whole idea of pornography as a sexual exercise will become increasingly heartbreaking as you continue to grow more and more like Christ.

One day, you realize that you are no longer fighting pornography because your new heart has stopped desiring it. Porn has become nothing more than a dusty pair of snowshoes sitting in your garage. Sure, you thought it was fun at one time, but you've found something so much better now. You've found the very thing your heart was looking for all along.

13 John Eldredge, *Wild at Heart* (Nashville, TN: Thomas Nelson Inc., 2011).

LIE #10

God Can No Longer Use Me Because of My Pornography Addiction

I may not have gone where I intended to go,
but I think I have ended up where I needed to be.
DOUGLAS ADAMS

When was the last time you came across a person you would consider to be crazy? No, I'm not talking about "crazy" Uncle Bill who comes downstairs on Christmas morning wearing nothing but briefs, slippers, and chest-hair while spouting off conspiracy theories about Nixon being a robot. I'm talking about someone who actually scares you because you sense there is something dangerous controlling their mind. Today, it's likely you've encountered someone like that at least once in your life.

This isn't a new problem. In fact, we see these people all throughout the Bible. The main difference is that the Bible recognizes the more extreme cases as spiritual oppression, whereas contemporary society tends to lump all of them together under the broad definition of mentally ill.[1] Sadly, because

1 I'm not saying all mental illness is demonic possession, although some of it most likely is. That discussion is far outside the scope of this book, though.

society has never had a good solution for how to handle these people, they are often driven away and forced to live as homeless wanderers.

Perhaps the most vivid illustration in the Bible of one of these people is the encounter Jesus had with the demon-possessed man in the region of Gerasenes.[2] This dude was crazy, and everyone knew it. We know the local townspeople were scared of his mental instability because they repeatedly tried to chain him up to keep him from hurting anyone. But the chains around his hands and feet weren't strong enough to stop his demonic rage. He repeatedly broke out of them, tore his clothes, and went right back to yelling and screaming. The Bible never tells us what specific things he would shout at people as they walked by, but it's probably safe to assume they were at least incoherent, and probably offensive and blasphemous.

I picture this man as a frightening spectacle. I imagine him with long, dirty hair and a huge, grizzled beard. I see strips of tattered clothing hanging loosely off his shredded body—shredded referring to his muscles as well as the wounds from his self-mutilation. I think of him as a real-life Incredible Hulk, screaming and throwing stones at anyone who came too close to him.

But no one ever did get close to him—at least not voluntarily. No one, except for Jesus.

When this man spotted Jesus walking by in the distance, he immediately ran toward Him shouting, "What do you want with me?" Try to picture that for a minute. If this dude started to come at me screaming, I'd turn and run for sure. Not Jesus, though. He just stands there calmly, recognizing the demonic nature of the man's condition, and exercises His authority over the demons. The evil spirits have no choice but to listen to Jesus, so they leave the man and enter into a herd of roughly 2,000 pigs, causing them to freak out, run into the lake, and drown.

The huge commotion brought many of the locals out to come and see what was going on:

> When they came to Jesus, they saw the man who had been possessed by the legion of demons, sitting there, dressed and in his right mind; and they were afraid (Mark 5:15).

---

2 Mark 5:1–20.

Jesus had set this man free from his bondage. He had made this man whole again. He had brought him back to life. And it freaked people out.

The townspeople didn't know what to make of this situation. They knew the insane power they had witnessed in this man, and now this Jesus guy had come with an even greater power. They didn't know if they could trust Him or not. I'm sure they were a bit ticked about the loss of all the pigs as well. That was a lot of bacon that just got wasted. So they did what many people do when they're afraid of something they don't understand—they formed a mob and ran Jesus out of town.

As Jesus was leaving, the formerly demon-possessed man came up to Him and begged to come along. Jesus had a different plan for him, though. He asked the man to stay where he was and share his story with those in his community.

Jesus didn't tell this man to wait until he became a "mature" believer. He didn't tell him to spend a certain amount of time studying his new faith before he would be ready. Jesus told the man to start sharing his Jesus story immediately after he was converted. Literally on the same day, if not the same hour. And you know what happened?

> The man went away and began to tell in the Decapolis how much Jesus had done for him. *And all the people were amazed* (Mark 5:20).

Jesus knew the best time for this man to begin sharing his story was right away. Something powerful had happened in his life that nobody would be able to deny. The townspeople—and probably many throughout the whole region—knew this man as the crazy guy in the cemetery. Yet here he was, cleaned up, wearing clothes, and obviously very different. And everyone wanted to know how. Because these people recognized his transformation could be nothing short of a miracle, they were more inclined to listen to him. And when he told them about how Jesus had set him free, they were amazed.

A few chapters later, we see Jesus returning to this same area, giving us great insight into the impact this one man was having on his community. As far as we can tell, no one else had trusted Jesus during that first visit.

In fact, they had run Him off. But now, only a few weeks later, He is welcomed by a huge crowd of over 4,000 people, all of whom were eager and excited to hear His teachings.[3]

Before this man was set free by Jesus, no one would have considered him capable of impacting others, especially for the kingdom of God. He was too crazy. Too messed up. Too far gone. But this one man, by sharing his personal story of how Jesus changed his life, influenced thousands of lives within a matter of weeks.

Chances are, you've at least considered the thought that God may have had big plans for you once. But not anymore. That ship has sailed. Maybe it's because of something you did in the past, or something that was done to you. Perhaps it's the accumulated effects of all the shame and guilt that come with addiction. Either way, you look at the path your life has taken and believe the lie that God can no longer use you.

No matter how bad your life has been, though, it's unlikely that you're worse than a guy possessed by an entire legion of demonic spirits. You probably aren't naked, covered in blood, living in a graveyard, spitting insults and abuse at everyone who wanders by. But even if you were, it still wouldn't matter. Jesus can still save you. And not only that, He can still use you as well. In fact, it seems as if He goes out of His way to find the least likely candidates to use in amazing ways to spread the good news of His kingdom to the world.

TRUTH: God loves to use broken people to do amazing things for His kingdom, regardless of their past.

Satan wants to convince people that their past has disqualified them from making an impact in this life. He will tell you that because of your mistakes, your addictions, your brokenness, God will no longer use you. He wants you to believe that God only calls perfect people, while at the same time reminding you that you are far from perfect.

3 This was the same crowd who was about to receive the miraculous all-you-can-eat buffet of fishes and loaves, which is how we know the specific number (Mark 8:1-8).

But if you are in Christ, you *are* perfect in God's eyes. In fact, the minute you place your faith in Christ, you are a new creation. And that's how God sees you. He no longer holds your sin against you. The stains of your past have been washed off your portrait hanging on God's wall, leaving a clean canvas for Him to paint His ideal future on.

Because of this, nothing from your past will ever be bad enough to disqualify you from the amazing future God has planned for you. Just look at God's prophecies to the Israelites through Jeremiah. For the first 28 chapters of the book, God lays out a list of all the ways the Israelites have turned away from Him. There's adultery and idolatry. They have listened to false prophets and allowed pagan practices to enter into their worship. The entire nation has hardened their hearts toward Him and rejected His ways.

As a consequence for their sins, God has allowed them to be taken into exile by the Babylonians. But even then, He doesn't give up on them. In the twenty-ninth chapter, He encourages them not to lose heart even while they remain in captivity. He calls them to set their eyes back on Him and warns them to not be deceived again. He encourages them that this period of exile will not last forever, and that He hasn't forgotten them. Then, in the midst of one of the lowest points in Israel's history, God makes this stunning promise to them:

> "I know the plans I have for you," says the LORD. "They are plans for good and not for disaster, to give you a future and a hope" (Jeremiah 29:11).

No matter how far the Israelites strayed from God, they would always be welcomed back into His good plan if they chose to trust Him again. And it's no different with you and me. Regardless of where you have been, He still has a plan for you. A plan with a future. A plan full of hope.

God Has Good Plans for Your Future

You may be reading this book with the sole purpose of finding freedom from pornography. That's great, but I'd like to encourage you to set your goals even higher. God's plans for you are bigger than just overcoming porn, so it only makes sense that yours would be as well.

God doesn't set you free just so you can enjoy your freedom in isolation. He sets you free so you can walk boldly into the calling He has for you without being shackled by sin and bondage. Or, to put it another way, He always sets you free *from* something *to* something. He frees you *from* your past in order to release you *to* the future He has for you.

One of the coolest things about all this is that He doesn't just throw out your past. He actually uses the events of your past—even the events you're certain will disqualify you—as building blocks for your future. I can look back at the events of my life now—even the hard ones—and see how God has been using them to prepare me for my calling to recovery ministry every step of the way:

- I remember having a desire to help other men find freedom from pornography as far back as high school, even while I was still in the grip of my own addiction.
- He led me to a job in publishing, providing the connections and knowledge of the industry that have opened doors for this book to exist.
- Because of some false accusations against me, I was required to undergo a year of sexual-addiction counseling. As difficult as that was at first, I quickly came to realize that God was using it to train and equip me to become a counselor myself.
- I lost my job at what appeared to be the most inopportune time. But now I can see how God took me out of that job to provide a way for me to become self-employed. This new freedom has given me the flexibility in my schedule to write this book, start my blog, and meet with guys whenever I need to.
- God has even used my pornography addiction to prepare me for my calling as a counselor. I know the struggles, the pain, the fear, and the isolation addicted men are going through because I've been there myself.

Instead of casting aside my past, God is using the lessons I learned from it to equip me for the life He has called me to. These painful situations have also given me a better perspective on my relationship with Christ. Because I have experienced the brokenness that came from my life falling apart, I am much more aware of how desperately I need Jesus to save me. I've experienced His love and grace in ways I never would have if I hadn't reached rock-bottom. If it weren't that my addiction had brought me to such a low point in my life, I would still be trying to save myself through being a good person. As crazy as it sounds, I'm actually thankful for my past—even the pornography addiction—because I now see how God has redeemed it for His glory. I see how He is using the events of my past for my good and the good of others, just as He promised He would.

In the same way, He has a plan to redeem your past mistakes and use the lessons you're learning from them to impact the world in miraculous ways.

God's Plans for You are Specific to You Alone

The entire course of your life has been preparing you for the calling God has created specifically for you. Because of this, no one else will ever be as qualified as you are to fulfill it. That's the amazing thing about your calling. It's *your* calling.

Although your calling is specific *to* you, it's never *about* you. Yes, when you walk in your calling, it will bring you happiness, fulfillment, and joy, but those are the benefits that come from following God, not the purpose of your calling. The purpose of your calling is to glorify God and point others toward Him. As Tony Evans says in his book *Destiny*:

> Your destiny is the *customized life calling* God has ordained and equipped you to accomplish in order to bring Him the greatest glory and achieve the maximum expansion of His kingdom.[4]

To put it even more simply, your calling will be about loving God and loving others.[5] But what does that look like in your life? How do you discover your specific calling and walk confidently in it?

---

4 Tony Evans, *Destiny* (Eugene, OR: Harvest House Publishers, 2013), 27.

5 Matthew 22:36–40.

God Has Already Given You Some of the Puzzle Pieces

You may not realize it, but the majority of what we've talked about up to this point has been providing clues about your specific calling. These truths about who you are and what you were created for are all relevant. In the same way a crossword puzzle becomes easier to complete after you write in a few of the words, recognizing these truths will make it that much easier for you to discover your calling. With that in mind, let's take a look at what we do know about it.

- *You already know who you are.* You are a child of God. And because you are in Christ, you know that God has made you a new person, with a new heart, and has already created good things for you to do.[6] Your calling will involve discovering what these good things are.

- *You already know where you are going.* Jesus repeatedly reminds us that we were created for eternity—not for this world. He warns us not to store up treasures here on Earth because they will rot away.[7] We are also encouraged to consider if the things we are investing our time in will survive into eternity.[8] Knowing this, you can see that your calling will always have an eternal perspective. It will be about investing in your eternal destination, not investing in things of this world.

- *You already know who empowers you.* God's calling for your life will far exceed anything you are capable of doing on your own. Further, He isn't going to call you to something without empowering you to do it effectively. This is why He has placed the Holy Spirit within you to give you all the wisdom, power, and self-discipline you will need to live out your calling.[9] By recognizing this, you can see that your calling will be something

6 Ephesians 2:10.
7 Matthew 6:19–21.
8 1 Corinthians 13:12–15.
9 2 Timothy 1:7.

> over and above what you could do on your own. It will require you to rely on the power of the Holy Spirit within you.

Your calling will be about fulfilling the good things that God has created for you to do, making an eternal impact that far exceeds anything you could do in your own power.

This understanding definitely gets us closer and narrows our focus, but it still doesn't answer the question of your *specific* calling. For that, we're going to need to look at how God tends to reveals His plans to us.

God Reveals His Plans for You One Step at a Time

Where we tend to get confused about our calling is when we focus on the big picture of our life as a whole while ignoring the day-to-day steps God is asking us to take next. We ask questions like "What is God's will for my life?" but rarely ask, "What does God want me to do *today*?" But He wants to have a relationship with you, and relationships require frequent connection and interaction or else they will die.

When we ask God to tell us His will for our life, what we are usually requesting from Him is a map that outlines exactly how to get from point A to point Z. If He were to reveal all of that to you, though, you would never need to check back in with Him regarding your next steps. That's why He is much more interested in walking with you from point A to point B. Once you reach point B, He will open the door to point C and walk with you there. And so on.

I love how David describes this daily dependency in Psalm 119:

> Your word is a lamp to guide my feet
> and a light for my path.[10]

David understood that walking with God is a lot like wandering down a dark trail with a lantern that illuminates only a small area around your feet. As you progress down the trail, the light continues to move with you, revealing just enough of the path so you can safely take your next step. If

10 Psalm 119:105.

David had had the daytime sun to guide Him, he could have wandered all day without consciously thinking about his dependency on the light. But because the lamp was so intimately tied to where he was, he had to remain with it to benefit from the light. If he had wandered away from the light, he would have stumbled or became lost. In the same way, we must remain with God and seek His next step for us if we are to continue down the path toward our calling.

There's a good chance that you are already sensing a specific step that God is asking you to take next. It may be the very first step of trusting Him *fully* with your life. It may be opening up about your addiction to someone. It may be repenting and turning away from a specific sin. Regardless of what it is, it's probably something He is putting on your heart that will require you to trust Him—to walk *with* Him.

We often reach points in our journey where the next step seems too difficult and look for alternate ways to keep moving forward. *Can I go from point A to point C and skip point B?* The answer is usually no. In fact, it's often these points where God is calling you to do the impossible in order to strengthen your trust in Him.

> Trust in the LORD with all your heart, and do not lean on your own understanding. In all your ways acknowledge him, and he will make straight your paths (Proverbs 3:5–6).

If you don't trust God and take the step He is asking you to take, you will continue to wander aimlessly. Your path will no longer seem straight and your calling will become harder to recognize. This is why you must trust His plan for you one step at a time if you want to keep moving forward.

I encourage you to keep accepting His invitation to walk with you to the next point on your journey—no matter how crazy or impossible it may feel. It's these many individual destinations that, over time, will eventually bring you to your destiny. After all, when you begin to trust God with the small steps, He will start to reveal to you even more of your calling.[11]

It may seem frustrating at first, but it's actually incredibly loving of Him

---

11 2 Corinthians 5:7.

to reveal things to us in this way. If He had told me three years ago that my calling would involve writing a book and sharing my story in front of large groups of men, I wouldn't have been able to handle that knowledge. It would have freaked me out. But by revealing His plans to me one step at a time and requiring me to trust Him more and more with each step, He helped me become comfortable with where I am today. I have learned that every step that brought me to where I am has been orchestrated and empowered by Him. And best of all, because I recognize He opens doors only when I'm ready to walk through them, I can look at where I am—wherever it might be—and trust that I am right on schedule.

God Reveals His Plans for You According to His Schedule

Maybe it's human nature in general, or maybe it's just a guy thing, but it seems like most people have a sense they should be further along in their goals than they actually are. Whether we feel we aren't climbing the corporate ladder quickly enough or we aren't as spiritual as we wish we were at this point in our life, we tend to feel like we're always behind schedule. But here's the amazing thing—God wanted this version of you, at this level of maturity, to be right where you are at this exact moment in time. As far as He is concerned, you're right on schedule.

The problem of feeling like we're behind schedule often comes because we're comparing ourselves to others. When we do this, we are rarely comparing apples to apples, however. We typically compare our outtakes to other people's highlight reels (Facebook, anyone?). So obviously, everyone else is going to appear to be much further along than we are. But God isn't calling you to be like Moses, Billy Graham, or Saint So-and-So. He's calling you to be you, because He created you to be you.

Nobody knows where you are and what you can handle right now better than God. So, doesn't it make sense to trust His schedule for you? I may want to have a blog with 10,000 followers who eagerly await my insights each week, but God knows the best thing for me right now is to have three readers—two of which are my parents. You may want to be completely free from pornography today, but maybe He knows it's better for you to slip up a few times a year to remind you how much you still need His help.

This doesn't mean you accept where you are and stop moving forward. God's schedule will always have you progressing toward sanctification. But it does mean that it's okay to not be perfect yet. It's okay to not have a huge platform of influence today. It's okay to start small, as long as you start—just as we see in Zechariah:

> Do not despise these small beginnings, for the LORD rejoices to see the work begin (Zechariah 4:10).

The key to accepting that you are on God's schedule is to stop focusing on what you think you *should* be doing for Him. Instead, focus on what He wants to do through you. I think I should be completely free from pornography before I write a book on finding freedom from it, but He has made it clear to me that He wants to work through me right now.

If you trust what God wants to do through you, no matter how small or insignificant it may seem, I guarantee you it will lead you deeper and deeper into your calling. And because His calling for you is perfectly aligned with His schedule for your life, you can trust that He already has created good things for you to do wherever you are now, regardless of how ready you may feel.

What Does This Have to Do with Pornography?

Remember, God doesn't want to set you free from pornography for your freedom alone. He wants to set you free so He can use your story to impact the lives of others. It may be large groups of men, or it may be a few close friends. Either way, it will happen, because the further you walk down this road to freedom, the more others will notice a change in you. This change will be amazing...and undeniable.

Other people will, at some point, start to ask what has caused this transformation in you, opening the door to some amazing conversations. When you take advantage of these opportunities to share your story with others, you shine the light of Christ for those who are still wandering in the darkness.[12] That's why Peter tells us to always be ready to share our reason for hope with anyone who asks.[13]

---

12 Luke 8:16.

13 1 Peter 3:15.

This desire to share your story with others will become a strong motivator for you to "walk in a manner worthy of the calling to which you have been called."[14] You will recognize that if you don't do this, no one will see anything in your life worth asking about. It won't disqualify you from your calling, but it will make it significantly harder to live it out. It's the equivalent of driving around with your emergency brake on.

I have found that when I am facing temptation, God often empowers me to walk away by reminding me of His calling on my life. *This is not who you are anymore. I've called you to something so much greater than this. I know you can walk worthy of your calling.* His gentle reminder causes me think of the men I am working with, the ministry He has entrusted me with, and the crippling effects that giving in to sexual temptation would have on all of it. I suddenly realize that it's simply not worth it to give in to the temptation.

You also can depend on God to remind you of your calling in your times of deepest struggle. You can ask Him to do this. His reminder will give you the strength to continue on in the fight. It will pull your focus off the desire for immediate gratification and place it back on the promise He has made to take care of all your needs for you.

You may want the details of your specific calling now. But as I said, that's for you and Jesus to figure out as you walk down the road of life together. You can depend on this, however: God will never hide your calling from you. He *wants* you to recognize the good things He has created for you to do.

> "I know the plans I have for you," says the Lord. "They are plans for good and not for disaster, to give you a future and a hope. In those days when you pray, I will listen. *If you look for me wholeheartedly, you will find me*" (Jeremiah 29:11–13).

I encourage you to seek after God with all your heart. If you look for Him, you will find Him—and discover His calling for you as well. It's His promise to you, and you can trust it.

---

14 Ephesians 4:1 ESV.

CONCLUSION

Where Do You Go from Here?

It's a dangerous business, Frodo, going out of your door...
You step into the Road, and if you don't keep your feet,
there is no knowing where you might be swept off to.

BILBO BAGGINS

I am a child of the '80s, if you haven't figured it out by now. And like a lot of boys from that decade, I grew up with a passion for G.I. Joes, Transformers, Legos, and Choose-Your-Own-Adventure books. But if there was one thing I'm willing to bet that *every* boy from my generation was into, it would have to be the movie *Karate Kid*.[1]

You could argue that no movie inspired boys from my generation more than *Karate Kid*. The story of an underdog maturing into a mighty warrior awakened something in our young male hearts. My friends and I would tie bandanas around our foreheads and wrap belts around our waists, pretending to be karate warriors. We would spend hours practicing crane kicks on the playground, imagining we were fighting the evil Cobra-Kai. At heart, every one of us wanted to learn how to be a warrior like Daniel-San.

In the movie, Daniel approaches an elderly Japanese man named

1 If you haven't seen the original *Karate Kid* yet, your life isn't complete. Go over to Netflix and watch it right away. I'll still be here when you get back. Trust me on this. You'll thank me.

Mr. Miyagi and asks him to teach him karate. Mr. Miyagi agrees, providing Daniel does whatever is asked of him without question. The boy agrees, but quickly starts to regret his decision. Instead of being taught how to fight, his time with Mr. Miyagi is spent painting fences, waxing cars, and sanding floors. He begins to wonder if the old man is only using him for free labor.

In a moment of frustration, Daniel asks Mr. Miyagi why he isn't teaching him karate like he promised. He responds by asking Daniel to show him "wax-the-car." As Daniel performs the hand motion he has done thousands of times while waxing the car, Mr. Miyagi throws a punch at him. Reflexively, the boy uses the same hand motion to block the attack. In that moment, Daniel realizes how these seemingly unrelated chores he had been doing were actually teaching him how to fight on an instinctive level. Even though he didn't realize it at the time, Mr. Miyagi had been teaching him karate all along.

The truths in this book may seem to be unrelated to your struggle with pornography addiction. Concepts such as understanding who you are in Christ or how God loves you unconditionally will sometimes appear to be no more helpful than learning how to wax a car—tempting you to give up out of frustration. Let me encourage you to keep trusting these truths of Scripture. Trust that Jesus—much like Mr. Miyagi—knows the tactics you will need to learn to be prepared for this fight better than you do.

Remember, the battle we are fighting and the enemy we fight against are real. But instead of scissor-kicks and dragon-punches, his favorite way to attack you is with lies. And the way to defend against these lies isn't with power—it's with truth:

- When he tells you that your addiction defines who you are, you block his punch by trusting who God says you are.
- When he insinuates that you are the only one dealing with pornography on this level, you dodge his false accusation by sharing your struggles with other trusted brothers.
- When he tries to drop-kick shame directly into your soul, it will glance off without a scratch if you are trusting God's unconditional love and acceptance of you.

- When he tries to convince you to accept an invitation back into his dojo through bitterness, you turn him down because you trust that your Sensei is taking the best care of you.
- When he insists that your mistakes have made you ineligible for the tournament, you take your spot in the ring proudly, trusting that Jesus believes you are ready.

Our training is never done, of course. If you want to be prepared for the fight, you must "paint the fence" and "wax the car" daily. And by that I mean practicing the art of trusting these biblical truths. The more you put your faith in them, the more they will become your automatic response to temptation. Your battles will no longer require you to fight in your own power because your trust in Jesus will lead you to realize that He has already set you free.

So embrace the truth…trust Jesus…and be set free.

This may be the end of the book, but it's not the end of the road.

This, my friend, is the trailhead.[2]

And you will know the truth,
and the truth will set you free.
— **JESUS CHRIST**[3] —

---

2 John Eldredge, *Wild at Heart* (Nashville, TN: Thomas Nelson Inc., 2011).

3 John 8:32.

ACKNOWLEDGMENTS

The men of *The Great Escape* groups—You thought for a second I was going to name names, didn't you? Don't worry, I won't. You may not realize it, but you guys impact my life just as much as I've had the honor of impacting yours. I couldn't do this life without you all. Your love and acceptance helps make it possible for me to live in the light. I love you guys.

Peter Shannon—Simply put, my ministry would not exist without you. You not only walked with me through my own healing, but you have taught me how to walk with others as well. I no longer think of you merely as my counselor… I consider you my friend.

Dr. Neil Anderson—God used your book *The Bondage Breaker* to open my eyes to the truth behind my addiction. But more importantly, He used it to show me how to find my freedom in Christ. I cannot thank you enough for your ministry and what it has meant in my life.

John Lynch—When you spoke at Men's Roundup back in 2011, it was as if God had wrapped His arms around me and said, "Listen up, my son, this is my message to you." Before that weekend, I had only dipped my toe into the waters of grace, but thanks to your story of the two roads, I was finally able to jump in and trust Him. Without your ministry, I would still be so busy trying to please Him that I would never have been able to write this book.

John Eldredge—You taught me that we are part of an epic story and opened my eyes to the adventure of faith. Most of all, you showed me what it means to be alive to Christ. Thank you, my friend.

Nate Larkin—When you recorded your testimony for I Am Second, I doubt you imagined some guy in Oregon would see it and have his life transformed. I still remember the feeling of watching it for the first time and thinking: *That's my story.* Thank you for your honesty, your transparency, and your willingness to allow God to use your past to impact my present.

The many friends who have given me advice and support along the way— Bob Welch, Tim Wallace, Terry Glaspey, Gene Skinner, Kimberly Shumate, Paul Gossard, Cory Verner, Luke Zedwick, Bryson Lewis, Andrew Enders, Steve Hill, Tracy Sims, and many others.

ABOUT THE AUTHOR

Stephen Kuhn has been leading recovery groups, speaking at college campuses, and providing free online counseling through Belt of Truth Ministries for more than three years. His passion is to allow God to use the story of redemption in his life to encourage other men to seek healing through the work of Christ as well.

Stephen lives in Oregon and has worked as a graphic designer within the publishing industry for over ten years, but has only recently discovered his love for writing. Like most native Oregonians, he enjoys a good rain shower and probably drinks too much coffee. He spends his weekends hiking, climbing, and skiing, but his greatest joy is playing dress-up with his daughter.

To learn more about Stephen's ministry, follow his blog, or find additional resources, please visit him at www.beltoftruth.com.

CPSIA information can be obtained at www.ICGtesting.com
Printed in the USA
BVOW03s1552030414

349612BV00006B/32/P

9 781630 470302